PETER PHILP

Antique Furniture
for the smaller home

GRAMERCY PUBLISHING COMPANY
NEW YORK

Contents

CHAPTER ONE

Introduction

THIS book is absurdly ambitious. It attempts to cover, very briefly, the history of furniture from the Middle Ages to the outbreak of the First World War; and not the work of one country alone, but that of many different lands.

The attempt is made in the hope that it may clear a little of the mystique that surrounds the subject, without pretending—as the women's magazines sometimes do—that the most wonderful bargains are to be picked up in junk shops by exercising nothing more than that indefinable quality usually called 'good taste'.

Taste is a very personal matter, and if it is not to degenerate into mere eccentricity, it ought to be based on knowledge and supported, when the occasion demands, by expert advice. My advice is far from being expert, but it may help the reader to distinguish the true expert from the self-styled.

No apology is offered for the historical approach. Although the idea is to cater for those who want antique furniture 'for the smaller home', an interest in the subject as a whole is taken rather for granted. Were I possessed of true missionary zeal, no doubt I would try to win over the uncompromisingly contemporary-minded, who are so wedded to modern Scandinavian design that one sometimes feels that King Alfred might just as well not have bothered to resist the earlier invasion from that direction. But this book is not for the man who hides behind the beechwood room-divider as soon as the subject of antiques is mentioned.

If he wants to erect an artificial barrier of that kind, he's welcome to it—and I am very far from being the one to convert him. Good antiques are hard enough to find without any competition from him, and for me, the dividing line between 'antique' and 'modern' is an arbitrary one, anyway. I like well-designed furniture of any period, including our own, and I come down heavily on the side of those who cheerfully blend the old with the new. In this matter, the articles in the women's magazines, that I was so patronizing about a few paragraphs ago, consistently do a very good job in advocating broad-mindedness.

There are some who value things merely because they are old, and despise anything they know to be modern. Others admire novelty for its own sake and reject maturity as old hat. These two points of view are opposed, not only to each other, but to my own.

If you simply want something that is hallowed by time, go out into the garden and pick up the first stone you see. It is older by far than any piece of furniture you will ever buy, and if you take a good look at it, it may even prove more useful and more beautiful than some of the bric-à-brac that clutters many a home.

Furniture of the eighteenth century, for example, ought to be valued, not because it happens to be a couple of hundred years old, but because conditions at that time were favourable for making it to a very high standard, and there were enough people of good sense about at the time to take full advantage of the fact. Many of them also had the perception to hang on to some, at least, of their old possessions—already 'antiques', even then—and mix them discreetly with the very latest creations of Mr Chippendale.

Yet Chippendale himself designed some veritable monstrosities. It is no use pretending that everything made in the Georgian period was fine and beautiful. Even if we confine our collecting to the very best that money can buy—and to do that would need an awful lot of money—it is still, I think, a mistake to try to keep a room strictly in one period. Set pieces of this kind nearly always fail, suggesting as they do a way of life so remote from our own that it is quite impossible to maintain the illusion. The smallest anachronism destroys it, and the owners themselves, when they walk into their homes in their twentieth-century clothes, are hopelessly out of place. If you really want to keep your mid-Georgian gem completely in period, you'll have to take to wearing a powdered wig.

The most pleasing rooms are always composite creations, the individual pieces harmonizing or sometimes contrasting with the background and the rest of the furnishings. A Gordon Russell chair can be perfectly at home beside an Adam fireplace, and a Regency sofa will live very happily in the company of a Restoration cabinet. As for the woods themselves, they mostly mellow to one shade of brown or another, and the greater the variety, the richer the effect. In many of the finest pieces, a combination of several different woods is employed to provide contrast, and even without this added refinement, any well-figured piece of timber offers a superb blend of colour-tones within itself. Good natural colours always go together. To reject a piece of furniture because it does not exactly 'match' another——because it is of another period or made from a different wood—is to admit to being so conditioned by the uniformity resulting from the evils of mass-production as to be unable to appreciate the infinite variety that natural materials, skilfully exploited, can provide.

When I speak of the 'evils of mass-production', I do not mean that such a system is necessarily evil in itself. Properly used, it can—and often does—provide excellent commodities at prices everyone can afford, whereas the made-to-order equivalent may cost a great deal more without actually being very much better in quality. Neither division of labour nor the use of machinery are new inventions, and many of the things which we prize today as antiques were in fact made with such aids to production. Chinese porcelain of the eighteenth century, for example, was mostly the product of combined effort by many pairs of hands, each performing its special function and making its own contribution, and the bulk of it was thrown on the potter's wheel, which is a piece of machinery, when all's said and done. As for furniture, the mechanical lathe was used for turning the legs of tables and chairs hundreds of years ago; a machine for bevelling mirrors had been invented before 1700; mechanical saws were in use before 1800, and a carving machine appeared shortly after. (Much of the wood-carving at Westminster was done by machinery, before 1850.)

The greatest evil resulting from mass-production is the attitude of mind which not only accepts a degree of uniformity in the resulting products as a contingency, but actively resents any departure from the norm. It is one thing to say, 'I don't mind fifty million Chevrolets all looking alike.' It is quite another to add, 'I strongly object to a custom-built Rolls-Royce because it is different from all the Chevrolets, and even different from other Rolls-Royces.'

No one *says* that, perhaps. But a great many people *think* it, privately, subconsciously. And when they bring their minds to bear on choosing furniture, they actually say something, *mutatis mutandis*, very like it. I have had people come to me, in all good faith, explaining that they are selling some uninteresting furniture—a bedroom *suite* or a dining-room *suite*. I am delighted to hear it because I hate the word 'suite' and all it connotes. They go on to say that they want my help in replacing the cast-offs with a few good pieces. We discuss the matter at some length, we make a tour of inspection of my galleries, and two or three items are tentatively selected. Madam then says she would like to see them close together, to see if they match. While the necessary fetching and carrying is being done, I try, as tactfully as possible, to make the point I am trying, with rather less tact, to make here. Madam agrees with all I say. Then she looks at the assembled group, and after much debating (mostly with herself, for I am a rotten salesman and I know what is coming, anyway) she regretfully decides that the table is a tone too dark to go with the chairs, or that the wardrobe is a decade too late to accord with the chest-of-drawers.

I once knew some people who spent many years and a great deal of money in assembling a collection of Queen Anne walnut. They were discriminating to a fault, but they chose some very lovely pieces. They were obsessed with the idea of 'matching up', because they intended that all these pieces would ultimately furnish one splendid room. At last, the room in question was made ready, at a great deal more expense. It was provided with a 'new' Inigo Jones fireplace, and the re-decoration even included replacing the ceiling. The great day arrived and the precious articles were stood reverently in position. A day or two later, they came to me with faces as long as Stradivarius violins. (A fiddle means something quite different in the antique business, or in any other business, these days.) I asked them what was wrong, and they told me the room looked terrible. Would I come and look at it, and do something—anything—to improve it?

I went, taking with me a small piece of satinwood furniture, entirely different in colour and in period from their walnut. I didn't mention its existence until I had duly inspected the room, which looked, not surprisingly, like a shop-window full of good quality reproductions, all made by the same firm and sprayed with the same shade of cellulose. Every piece was perfectly authentic, of course, but everything matched so perfectly that the result was much too good to be true. I'm glad to say that the little bit of satinwood worked wonders.

If you intend furnishing your home, at least in part, with

antiques, do try to avoid catching what someone has aptly called the 'disease of suiteitis'. The thing to fear is not that your pieces won't match, but that they may match too closely, and instead of that charming interior you have dreamed about, you can easily end up with a stuffy, cheerless monotony.

Another prevalent phobia concerns the placing of antique furniture in a modern house. Agreed that a vast number of so-called 'traditional' houses being built today are so box-like, so lacking in character that it is not very easy to furnish them in an interesting way; even so, many owners of the three-up, two-down type of semi-detached seem to me to take a terribly defeatist attitude by resigning themselves to those standard items of equipment which manufacturers deem the only suitable adjuncts to a domesticity that gives pride of place to the motor car, the television set and the washing machine.

I am all for having any gadgets that compensate for living in an age dominated by the fear of the niftiest gadget of all, i.e. the hydrogen bomb. On the other hand, I flatly refuse to let their modernity preclude my enjoyment of what has survived from past ages which were, in their day, terrorized by fears of the plague, the French fleet and all the other recurring threats that did not stop our ancestors from making, and enjoying, beautiful things.

Modern houses may not provide the *ideal* setting for antique furniture. All the more reason, then, for introducing a few care-fully chosen pieces to give grace where there would otherwise be only oafish utilitarianism, and to remind us that we have a past worth preserving against the marauding present and the predatory future.

I must confess that I have benefited, in a selfish way, on more than one occasion, from the mistaken idea that the small modern house is no place for antiques. Many times I have been asked to buy the only decent pieces of furniture in the place 'because they don't fit in here'. As often as not, these rejects are the only pieces that would, carefully placed, make the house into a home, but even when I say so—against my own interests—the owners refuse to consider the idea. They prefer to discard their heirlooms to make room for some nondescript junk. With mixed feelings, I make out the check. One function of the dealer is to transfer good things from the homes of those who don't appreciate them, or can't afford to keep them, to the homes of those who do and can. The most he can do is try to be fair to the seller and honest with the buyer.

The commonest. reason for discarding a piece as unsuitable for a modern house—or for rejecting it when it is offered for sale—is that it is too large. Now this book is supposed to be about antique furniture for the smaller home, but that doesn't necessarily mean that it is about small furniture. There is a great vogue for dainty little bits and pieces, and many people with large, well-proportioned rooms seem to prefer to clutter them up with a series of small articles, rather than dignify them with the larger, more imposing items. Many homes would look infinitely better if the number of fussy little things were cut down in favour of one or two well-designed, substantial, useful pieces.

Some friends of mine, who live in a small bungalow, were bequeathed a splendid Sheraton sideboard, some seven feet in length and two-and-a-half feet in depth. They were determined to use it somehow, but it was physically impossible to place it in their tiny dining-room. Undaunted, they re-papered the end wall of the sitting-room with a very lush flock-paper, and placed the sideboard against it. It fills the entire wall, it breaks all the accepted rules of what ought to fit into a small room, it has nothing in common with the rest of the furniture except quality, and yet it looks absolutely wonderful. Most people, faced with such a gift horse, would not even have stopped to look it in the mouth before telephoning frantically to the nearest dealer or auctioneer.

Another standard worry that deters many from keeping such pieces as they inherit is bad condition, especially the presence of wood-worm. Provided that too much damage has not already been done, wood-worm can be dealt with very effectively by the amateur, the insecticides on the market now being most efficient if both insecticide and patience are generously employed.

Skilful repairs are not, usually, a do-it-yourself job, and it is not always easy to find the right man to undertake them. It is dangerous to *buy* pieces in a bad state of repair, unless you know someone who can be relied upon to put them into good order. It is better by far to go to the better type of dealer with skilled men in his own workshops who can effect any necessary repairs, and to pay that much more for the piece that needs no attention. But if, as so many people do, you inherit some furniture of good lineage but in shabby state, do make every effort you can to save it and use it in your home, before sending it off to the sale-room. There, it will not look very prepossessing to the general public, and 'the trade' will probably buy it for rather less money than the better kind of dealer would pay you for it privately.

Sale-rooms exercise a great fascination for some people, and a study of auction-prices is a valuable guide for the would-be collector. But it is very definitely the kind of place where the fools-rush-in principle operates at full pressure. In a public auction, you buy at your own risk, and you have nothing like as much redress as you have in buying from dealers of good standing, who are usually prepared to give a worth while guarantee and have a reputation to maintain. Never buy in auction unless you really know what you are doing, or have someone with expert knowledge to advise you.

Try to acquire a little knowledge for yourself before blindly placing confidence in someone else. So many well-meaning people go around giving gratuitous advice which is taken on trust by those even more ignorant than themselves. Often I have been shown some worthless object which the poor, deluded owner really believes to be valuable, because 'the doctor (or the vicar, or the man next door) said it was a genuine antique—worth a lot of money, he said . . .'

Well, the old boy meant no harm. Wanted to cheer her up at a difficult time, or impress her with his knowledgeability; perhaps he even believed it. To implant a false sense of values is so easy, but though it may seem harmless at the time, sooner or later someone is almost sure to have the sad task of disillusioning the little old lady, who will make it pretty plain that she regards him as a rogue and a liar, nothing and no one being able to come between her and her steadfast loyalty to the doctor, the vicar, or the man next door.

One does not become a really good judge of antiques by making wild guesses at the merits of one's friends' possessions, by spending twenty minutes annually in a curio-shop in a seaside town during a shower of rain, or by casually glancing through one or two books like this one. It is only achieved at all by giving up a good deal of time and thought to the subject, and by putting theoretical knowledge to the test of practical experience whenever and wherever possible.

On the theoretical side, it is essential to master certain terms of reference. The first definition to be learned, obviously, is what constitutes an antique. For most purposes, it is a man-made object at least one hundred years old, but various official and semi-official authorities make their own rules. Most countries permit authentic antiques to be admitted free of duty, but whereas the Union of South Africa, for example, and Australia accept the hundred-year definition, the United States of America require an article to have been made prior to 1830 if it is to enter the country as a duty-free antique.

Agreement is not complete even within 'the trade'. Anything more than a hundred years old can be exhibited at the Kensington Antiques Fair, for instance, but at the time of writing, the earlier date of 1830 is insisted on at the Chelsea Fair, conducted only a couple of miles away, with many of the same dealers exhibiting at both and certainly a great many of the same customers patronizing them.

The stricter interpretation seems to be based on the assumption that 1830 marked the death not only of George IV but of good design and craftsmanship as well. I think it is also partly due to the curious fact that, while so much scholarship has gone into the study of the earlier periods that fairly accurate dating of their products is possible, it is only now that the middle and later nineteenth-century work is beginning to be taken at all seriously, and a great many good judges who can date furniture made at any time between Elizabeth I and the Regency with ease and certitude are on much less firm ground when dealing with things that first appeared about the time of the Great Exhibition.

I have already confessed that I do not worry over-much about the distinction drawn between 'antique' and 'modern'. By that, I do *not* mean that it doesn't matter whether a piece that purports to be an antique is genuine or not. I think it matters a great deal. What I *do* mean is that I refuse to shut my eyes to the possible merits of an article that, quite clearly, does not fit itself into either of the official categories.

But I make my living as an antique-dealer, and, as a writer on the subject, even I have to impose some sort of demarcation line and decide what should properly come within my province, catholic though I make it, and what should not. For most of us, there is a sort of half-formed idea that anything made in, and characteristic of the world as it was before we were born into it is, if not an 'antique', at any rate a 'period piece'. We may treat such things as a bit of a joke when older people recall them, but we are fascinated by them, nevertheless, and sometimes become enthusiastic about them. Think of the way that young people of today regard silent films and veteran cars.

Because I was born in 1920, I feel this sort of sentiment towards life as it was lived before the First World War. Officially, during business hours, I follow protocol and do not employ the term 'antique' to cover anything later than early Victorian; but privately I cannot help applying this 'before-my-time' sense of the past to anything made up to 1914 or thereabouts. If I want to rationalize my attitude, I do so on the grounds that modern life and modern methods may be said largely to date from then on.

But really, it is a personal point of view, and it is the one from which this book is written. You may share it, now, or you may come to share it with me before the end, if you ever get there. It's an indefensible attitude, of course, which really says, 'An antique is something that's older than I am.' An elderly lady once pointed to a piece of furniture in my home and asked if it was an antique. 'Not quite,' I said, 'it's about ninety years old.' She looked at me contemptuously. 'I'm ninety-three myself,' she proclaimed, 'and I *certainly* don't think of myself as even *remotely* antique.'

If I had said the thing was just over a hundred years old, and therefore an antique, she would, I feel sure, have accepted it without a qualm. Anything just a few years before one's own appearance on the scene has all the charm of period-stuff; anything made just after belongs to one's own day and age, and is therefore 'modern'.

Wrong-headed I may be, but I feel sure that this relating of self to time and its products has a deeper significance than the pronouncement of any government or trade organization as to what constitutes an antique.

At all events, I shall carry the story of furniture beyond the limits usually set in books on antiques proper, for the benefit of those who, like myself, regard Edwardiana, as well as Victoriana, with affection if not reverence.

From a practical point of view, too, there is much to be said for making a study of the later nineteenth and earlier twentieth centuries. It was then that the best quality reproductions of furniture of the classic periods were made, and these pieces are now mature enough to deceive the eyes of quite shrewd judges. To my certain knowledge, at least one Edwardian copy of an Adam commode failed to be detected for what it was, a year or so ago, and was sold under the eyes of so-called experts as an eighteenth-century piece at a price exceeding $3,000.

The flaw in the judgement of so many people is a total reliance on the recognition of style. Now, a knowledge of style is very valuable, and indeed, it is about all that can be gleaned from book-learning alone. It is the one essential that can be grasped by private study, especially of good photographs. But of course, it is not enough by itself. A really skilful fake is often accurate enough, so far as style is concerned—though it's surprising how many fakers fall down even as to obvious details of design.

A really competent judge of furniture must have some practical knowledge of woodwork—how things were put together at different periods, what timbers were used, what tools were employed. He asks himself whether the veneers, if any, are of the right thickness—and what of the glue, the nails and screws, the methods of jointing and of polishing? Are there signs of wear where one might expect them? If not, is it because the piece is not old enough to exhibit them, or because legitimate repairs have been carried out? And if such signs *are* exhibited, are they authentic or have they, too, been faked?

I cannot hope to give you, within the pages of this book, a very clear idea of how to answer these questions in any given case. I can only advise you to ask them, to train yourself to find out by observation and experiment, and if you are not satisfied, either with the piece or the person who is selling it, to leave it where it is.

When I speak of legitimate repairs, the operative word is 'legitimate'. So often, what is passed off as a 'repair' is in fact a discreet bit of faking to make an old but unimportant article into an item for the collector who likes to think of himself as 'advanced', but who yet lacks the knowledge needed before buying from unreliable sources—especially when a premium is being placed on rarity value.

If the price asked is, after all, no greater than that of a modern equivalent or brand new reproduction, no great harm can befall the buyer. The thing is still worth the money as a furnishing piece, and if it turns out to be nothing more than that, it can always be sold at no heavy loss. But to be carried away by the rarity value and the alleged importance of a piece of furniture that may well have been cleverly got up to appeal to the eye of the bargain hunter in some out-of-the-way shop or sale-room—that is really to court trouble. The most dangerous circumstances of all, perhaps, are those surrounding the purchase of a piece in some elegant flat. The owner usually advertises in the morning papers—the classier ones, of course—and invariably he is going abroad. The things are offered at sacrificial price for a quick sale, and the phrase 'no dealers' often occurs.

If you answer an advertisement like that, you really deserve to finish up as the proud owner of a four-poster bed that Elizabeth slept in, the watch that Marie Antoinette wore to the gallows, and Dr Johnson's very own personal teapot. Whenever 1 am offered items like these, I always say that I'm overstocked with that particular commodity. What is called 'association value' is usually extremely difficult to support with valid evidence, and without it, the article must stand or fall on its own merits, irrespective of the legend, however romantic it may be in its appeal.

I know buyers of antiques who rely on some mysterious faculty called flair, instinct, 'nose' or a sixth sense. Undoubtedly, some people have it, whatever it is. Sometimes, it leads them to really exciting discoveries, of which they boast, quite modestly, for the rest of their lives; and sometimes it prompts them to land themselves with the most awful stumers, about which their friends hear very little. Personally, I distrust instinctive buying that is not supported by a good, sound knowledge of the subject.

However, there *is* an instinct that can work very well in a negative way, and save one from making a dreadful mistake when common sense gives the signal to go ahead. Pieces of furniture are very like people, in that they have character that can be described in human terms. They even seem to me to have sex. There are masculine and feminine pieces, and pieces which are modest or belligerent, vulgar or refined, blasé or naïve, honest or otherwise. Fake things, having been made by fraudulent people, certainly seem to take on something of the personality of their creators. One learns to distrust certain pieces on sight, however engaging their manner, just as one would suspect their makers, if one were ever to meet them.

This sort of feeling for the character of furniture is part-instinct, part-experience, part-learning. I don't think it can be acquired by reading alone, but just as a good deal about life can be gleaned from the pages of a great novel or the lines of a fine play, so something of the right attitude to the subject can be got, I hope, even from a very informal approach like this—not that any attitude can really be said to be the 'right' one. There are many attitudes towards the collecting of antiques, and they are all 'right' in some sense or other.

This is not a reference book. There are really enough of those on the market already, and a short bibliography will be found on p. 165. It is a book for those who would like to know a bit about old furniture, and apply it to the furnishing of their homes.

I would stress the word 'homes'. Some people get so enthusiastic about antiques that, compared with their houses, the British Museum is positively cosy. Unless you really want to be an eccentric recluse, don't let it happen.

CHAPTER TWO

Gothic to Renaissance

IT may be whimsical to suggest, as I have done in the Introduction, that some pieces of furniture reflect the personalities of the people who made them, but even if you dismiss that as too fanciful, it is certainly true that they often tell us a great deal about the people for whom they were made.

Of all the influences that combine, at any given time, to dictate the trend of design, it is social pressure—the compulsion to keep up with the Jones'—that is one of the most powerful. It is surprising how very little furniture is really essential, and how much has been made to enhance the owner's status rather than increase his comfort. In many an African village, the stool that serves the chief as a throne is the only piece of furniture for miles around. The chief would be more comfortable sitting on his haunches, but he has to boost his ego and get the edge on the witch-doctor somehow. The same principle applies in what is laughably known as 'Western Civilization', where large organizations, both commercial and civil, enforce a strict grading system specifying exactly what furnishings an executive may have in his office. I know of one such hierarchy where the lowest level is permitted only a whitewood table and chair on bare boards, while the highest achieves the last word in room-at-the-topmanship with an office furnished entirely with antiques and Persian rugs.

In the private house, there is of course no written rule that permits Mrs Smith of Sutton Coldfield to have a genuine reproduction Tudor cocktail bar in her lounge, while forbidding Mrs Brown of Lexington, Ky., the luxury of a ten-foot bedstead with Corinthian columns in green marble at the corners; yet both these ladies know, in their secret souls, just what is permitted to them, tacitly, by protocol. They know it is all right to go one better than the neighbours whose husbands earn the same salary as their own, but to go two better is to run a grave risk of being ostracized on coffee-mornings.

In other words—snobbishness, pure and simple, with very little harm in it, and possibly quite a bit of good resulting! If the competitive spirit prompts people to beautify their homes

(not to mention stimulating the antique-trade, home and export)
I'm all for it. And it would be quite wrong to suppose that this
sort of thing is merely a symptom of modern decadence. It has

FIG. 1

English Oak of the Late Gothic Period
Mid-Sixteenth Century

A. Box-seated arm-chair.
B. Trestle table.
C. Iron hinge and lock plate.
D. Chest showing a different type of carved decoration in each of three
    panels; in actuality, the designs would be arranged symmetrically.
E. Solid-ended stool.

been going on for a very long time indeed. It has provided one of the most valuable stimuli to the making and collecting of fine things. My dictionary tells me that the original meaning of 'snob' was 'shoemaker'. I'm surprised it wasn't 'furniture-maker'.

To demonstrate that this really is an historic principle and not just a petty piece of personal cynicism, it is necessary only to consider the development of the chair—an article which those of us who live mainly sedentary lives have come to regard as a basic necessity. By custom and usage, that is what it has become, but the example already given of the African perched on his stool suggests that the original purpose, in primitive society, was to be, literally, 'one up'—about one foot up—above the rest when all were in a sitting position.

The stool was largely ousted, as a status-symbol, early in Northern European history, though in Italy, it took on grand forms and served as a seat of honour. The Doge of Venice, for example, used a type of stool as a judgement-seat. In Britain, the stool was a relatively humble article, normal seating for the less important people.

In its Gothic form, it was supported on a pair of shaped end-supports, joined together by a stretcher below that penetrates them, projects beyond them and is held in position by wedges (Fig. 1). The top is often hinged, with a box-like compartment such as we have in the modern music-stool. This box became gradually shallower and was eventually discarded as a feature. The solid end-supports were ultimately replaced by four turned legs. This later type is described on p. 58.

In according the important person a seat commensurate with his social standing, the Early English really went to town. One might be forgiven for expecting a stool with a back tacked on, making it into a primitive sort of chair. Not on your life! It was ages before anything as simple and logical as a nice little chair with a back and no arms was to develop. In the Middle Ages, the great ones were provided with something much more like a throne than a chair, having a seat of box-construction, a high, solid back, and equally solid arms (Fig. 1). Even in the great halls, there were seldom more than three chairs—one for the lord, one for his lady-wife, and possibly another, held in reserve for a visiting V.I.P.

Any entertainment was provided by the resident jester or

strolling minstrel, for whom a space was made in the great hall by taking the table to pieces when the meal was done. Life in feudal England was lived, to a large extent, communally, and the lord and master sat at high table, with his pretty wife on one side of him and a philandering knight on the other, making eyes at her across the gold plate. Apart from the afore-mentioned jester or minstrel, that was about the only amusement available after dark. Today, we have television, with jesters telling the same jokes they told then, otherwise things are much the same. Tables, however, have undergone a series of changes.

The type of dining-table in general use until late Tudor times was a massive affair consisting of oak boards joined together and resting on movable trestles. Reproductions of these, duly scaled down, abound, but few genuine examples come on to the market, and as nothing less than a moated grange will happily accommodate one, a book about antiques for the smaller home need hardly devote much space to the subject. To understand what came after, it is necessary to have some idea of what went on before, otherwise the mighty table of the so-called Gothic period would not get a mention here.

The term 'Gothic' is a misleading one, in that it really has little to do with the German tribes who tended to over-run much of Europe following the collapse of the Roman Empire. The Goths reached the zenith of their power in Spain, in the sixth century. By the beginning of the eighth, that power had been destroyed. What is called 'Gothic' art and architecture did not begin until the twelfth century. It originated in France and flourished throughout Europe for the best part of four hundred years. The confusion seems to have been started by a pupil of Michelangelo who wanted to be as offensive as possible about the buildings erected in the Middle Ages, and attributed them to the Goths who, so far as his native Italy was concerned, had never been more or less than a bunch of savage marauders.

Michelangelo's bright-eyed boy was concerned with praising what was then the new movement in architecture, which we call the Renaissance, and the classical forms on which it was based, at the expense of the merely old-fashioned. This is a little trick still beloved by exponents of most new art forms. Quite often, it works, and it worked then. It was not until the eighteenth century that enthusiasts like Horace Walpole began to re-discover the beauty of Gothic work, and even then their enthusiasm tended to become misplaced—but that can wait until we come to review its consequences.

For the moment, all that matters is that 'Gothic' is an inaccurate but useful term, first meant as one of abuse, but now used to embrace that splendid, soaring, decorated style of building that most of us associate with cathedrals having pointed archways and rose windows.

Much of the furniture that survives from the Middle Ages —and there really isn't a great deal—shows the Gothic influence in a marked way. No doubt this is partly because it is in churches that early pieces have been best preserved from the ravages of war, everyday use, smoke and heat from the hearth, drunken husbands, fashion-conscious wives, destructive children, brokers' men, cigarette ends, spilled drinks, amateur restorers and all the other dangers that threaten domestic furniture. (When you take them all into account, it's astonishing that there *is* any antique furniture.) Add to this the fact that, until about 1500, there wasn't much domestic furniture anyway, life being too insecure to make its accumulation worth while, and it will be seen that ecclesiastic pieces offer the best, and almost the only, scope for study. The chances are, however, that anything really worth calling domestic furniture at all followed fairly closely the pattern set by the churches. (Plate I).

Like the buildings, Gothic furniture was solidly constructed and richly decorated—not only by elaborate carving but with painting in primary colours, and gilding. What are now dignified, sombre pieces of oak must once have presented a positive carnival of colour.

Favourite motifs of the Gothic wood-carvers were foliage and flowers, with an occasional grotesque monster, within geometrically contrived spaces formed by setting a circle in a pointed arch. Perhaps the most characteristic feature of the period, both for the panelling of rooms and for furniture, was the 'linenfold' treatment of flat surfaces, as we now call it, though originally this formal, carved decoration was probably meant to represent scrolls of parchment (Fig. 1D).

It really became possible to use it, extensively, only after a revolutionary advance in construction. Until about 1400, joinery had consisted of pegging or nailing solid boards to one another in the simplest manner, which we call 'plank construction'. Shortly after that date, some unknown, enterprising Dutchman invented *framed* construction, whereby a panel of wood was loosely set in a framework of thicker timber, the loose fit allowing a margin of safety that reduced the risk of splitting if the timber should warp or shrink unequally. The relative thinness of the panel also helped to make furniture lighter in weight. All this required craftsmanship of a much higher order than had previously been needed, as plank construction had involved little

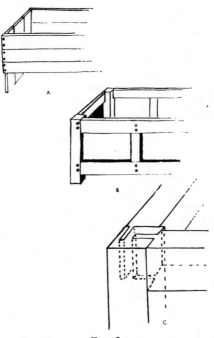

FIG. 2

Development of Constructional Methods
A. Plank construction.
B. Frame construction.
C. Tenon and mortise joint.

more than pinning or nailing the end, say, of a chest to the boards that comprised its front, whereas the horizontals of the frame construction had to be joined to the uprights, or 'stiles', by means of a tenon, or tongue, fitting into a mortise, or cavity. Women readers and others who get dispirited when presented with mild technicalities of this sort had better take a look at Fig. 2 and then forget the whole thing. As it happens to be one of the most important constructional developments in the history of furniture, I felt I ought to mention it, in passing.

The old, crude method was not, of course, abandoned at once, and though craftsmen all over Europe were fairly quick to follow the lead of the Low Countries and build furniture according to the new principle, in outlying places where traditions always linger on, chests, especially, continued to be made in the outmoded way. You are quite likely to come across a specimen of plank construction in the form of a chest made of ash, elm or oak, and the smaller ones, being only three feet or so in length, have a natural place in the country cottage; but do not assume that you have necessarily discovered a fourteenth-century primitive, just because it boasts plank construction. I don't mean that it may be a fake; although that is always possible, it is unlikely in this case, as simple chests are too commonplace for a good fake to be really profitable. But there is a very good chance that it may have been made in some remote, conservative spot, perhaps as late as 1600 or even later.

In fact, there is not much furniture earlier than, say, 1550 to be found outside churches and museums, and in England, at least, there has, for some years past, been only a limited interest in really early pieces. Before the First World War, there were far more serious collectors of old oak than there are today, and for the larger pieces especially, prices were higher then than they are now. On the continent of Europe, the situation is rather different. The Dutch and the Belgians are now systematically buying every interesting early piece they can find, and while the English, French, and American buyers concentrate on eighteenth and early nineteenth century elegance, Holland and Belgium are quietly investing in the work of the more remote periods. As it was the Low Countries that developed much of it in the first place, there is a certain poetic justice in the process. Many pieces which came to Britain from the Netherlands, or that were made here at that time in imitation of Dutch models, are now returning to their birthplace after a lapse of four hundred years or so.

Another example of sixteenth-century Dutch ingenuity which was much copied elsewhere was the draw-leaf table. With the passing of feudalism in England, the old, communal way of life in castles and fortified manor houses gave way to a pattern of living based more exclusively on the family proper. Under Elizabeth I, a middle class of merchants and independent trades-people emerged and consolidated itself, built houses that were relatively small and in which, at least in the larger towns and cities, the master and his family segregated themselves from the servants. (The old tradition persisted longer in the country.) The old business of who should sit at high table, who should be placed above, and who below, the salt—all this became out of date. Class distinction was now much simpler. You sat down to eat either with the family, or else in the servants' hall or kitchen. The trades-people were more fussy about such things than the old barons had been. It is not difficult, after all, to see why the word 'snob' changed its meaning as it did.

The consequence of this social reconstruction was a demand for more furniture of rather different types. The old trestle tables which had been set at right angles to each other in the Middle Ages, in much the same way as caterers marshal them today for wedding receptions and public banquets, were hopelessly unsuited to an arrangement whereby the household was divided at mealtimes into family and staff.

The first solution to the problem was provided by a table with a solid but movable top set on a framed-up stand, having four legs, usually bulbous in shape and ornately carved. These bulbous legs are known as 'cup-and-cover', because they strongly resemble the splendid silver-lidded cups of the period (Fig. 3). Turning on the lathe had now been learned in Britain—or rather, revived again after a lapse of centuries. (Many elaborate wood-working techniques had been known during the Roman occupation, but lost in the period of near-savagery that followed its termination.) Some of the legs on Elizabethan tables, however, are so Falstavian in their central girth that they could not be turned from one piece of wood. The leg was therefore turned, leaving a flat-sided section at the centre which was then built out and shaped to give the rotundity that accorded with the taste of the time.

FIG. 3

'Cup-and-Cover' Shapes in Silver and Wood
England, late sixteenth century
A. Silver standing cup-and-cover.
B. Silver-shape applied to turning a table-leg.
C. The same form applied to a bed-post.

This is the type of table popularly known as 'refectory', but in fact the monasteries had taken a bad knock some years before, from Henry VIII, and most of the tables of the kind that survive did not furnish the refectories of the monks at all, but the rooms of rich merchants.

It was this type of four-legged table which the Dutch adapted so that it should take up less space when not in use as a dining-table. The frame remained fixed, the legs being tied top and bottom by rails. The top had nearly always been made so that it could be lifted off, and the method now adopted was to fit under it, at each end, an extension that would slide out and be supported on bearers, the main table-top dropping automatically into position between them. There is really no point in giving an elaborate account of this mechanism, as millions of modern draw-leaf tables are still being constructed on exactly the same principle; indeed, most of the gadgetry to be found in present-day design was first thought of a long time ago.

For example, among the many treasures that were yielded up by the tomb of Tutenkhamen was a very useful bed that folded into three sections. A form of springing was provided by inter-laced cords or thongs, and the feet were of the kind we call 'claw-and-ball'—very popular with us in the eighteenth century, and still a firm favourite.

In the Middle Ages, people slept in bunks of one kind and another, built into the walls of the great halls and curtained off to give some degree of privacy. This principle of treating a bed as a sort of room-within-a-room persisted, in most countries, for centuries, in varying forms of tester and half-tester beds. The Italians had a type without any kind of canopy as early as the sixteenth century, but continued to employ the half-tester as well. In Britain, the four-poster dominated sleeping arrangements for about half a millenium. The earlier version was a crude, wooden construction that relied for its effect on rich hangings that were highly valued, but from late Tudor times onwards, the woodwork itself was often exposed and given decorative treatment by means of turning and carving. The posts of Elizabethan beds strongly resemble the legs of the tables described above, having cup-and-cover turnings, surmounted by capitals inspired by those of classical columns (Fig. 3).

This sort of treatment signifies a very important change from the Gothic style. It was the outcome of the Renaissance in Italy, filtering northward. English furniture at the end of the sixteenth century was still largely Gothic in feeling, with overtones of the Renaissance foisting themselves on to the native tradition in a rather brash way that suited the new-rich element in Elizabethan England very well. Few of us, buying for our own homes, are likely to encounter anything much earlier, and rather than devote more space to an academic discussion of the few other types of article that existed in the sixteenth century home, I would prefer to consider the forms they took in the next age, which has much to offer that is of practical value to the homemaker—even the impecunious one.

CHAPTER THREE

Renaissance to Baroque

I HOPE these chapter headings aren't too off-putting for those to whom terms like 'Gothic', 'Renaissance', 'Baroque' and so on are vague descriptions they have heard applied to draughty buildings by boring guides. The advantage of borrowing these words from architecture is that, when applied to furniture, they really *are* a little vague, in a way that gives the boring guide—in this case, myself—a chance to be discursive.

Although, as I have said in the Introduction, I do not much favour furnishing-schemes which try to be too faithful to a period, in writing a book of this kind it is simpler for everyone if some kind of chronological sequence is followed. If it is being written entirely from a national viewpoint, concerning itself only with the furniture of one country, to be read only by the people who live in it, then the author can chop up his text into convenient chunks with familiar names and dates. If it is written in English, for English and American readers and is devoted to English furniture, then phrases like 'The Early Stuart Period' or simply '1600-1650' make adequate sub-titles.

The difficulty is that books about antiques are read by a cosmopolitan public—or the author fondly hopes they will be—and this one attempts, however superficially, to take account of the furniture of other countries besides Great Britain, partly because it is impossible to understand English furniture without some reference to foreign influences, and partly because there will surely be some readers, even among the English themselves, who want to take an interest in the work of other nations besides their own.

To divide the story of furniture up, and label the divisions according to the course of English history, thus becomes too confusing a business altogether, if only for the reason that certain dominating influences were operating much earlier in some countries than in others.

That which we call the Renaissance began in Italy in the fifteenth century and only affected Britain, directly and indirectly, about a hundred years later. In the main, the influence was transmitted indirectly via the Low Countries, but there was perhaps rather more direct influence than is popularly supposed. For example, Henry VIII brought Italian craftsmen to work at Hampton Court on rooms intended for Anne Boleyn's use. The fact that she had been beheaded before the work was completed was her sad misfortune. Certainly, in the literary sphere, there was a lively interest in Italian writing. Shakespeare is known to have pinched more than one of his plots from Italian sources, and during the reign of Elizabeth I, some seven hundred Italian manuscripts were translated into English.

During the hundred years that elapsed between 1450 and 1550, the course of world history was radically changed by widely differing causes. To attempt to enumerate them and explain them is beyond the scope of this book, not to mention the ability of its author. They included events as seemingly disparate as the fall of the Eastern Empire, the invention of the printing press, the discovery of America, and the Sack of Rome. They led to powerful movements such as the Reformation and the Counter-Reformation. They saw the re-birth of learning in general, a re-awakening of interest in the arts, and especially the artistic values of the ancient Greek and Roman cultures. All this, or rather the net result of this, was the flowering of thought and skill which we call the Renaissance.

Part of the impetus undoubtedly came as the consequence of a disaster to Christendom: the seizing of Byzantium (Constantinople) by the Turks in 1453. This meant that Rome was now the centre of the Christian faith, and into Rome there flocked many refugees from the capital of the Eastern Empire, bringing with them not only many treasures from Byzantium, but also the skills that had gone into their making. The Roman Church was itself weak to the point of near collapse, and Italy was divided into quarrelling states, all of them the potential prey of watchful Europe. Yet out of this confused picture there emerged a splendid upsurge of creative talent that manifested itself in painting such as the Western world had never seen, architecture that set out to rival and even surpass the achievements of the ancients, and magnificent examples of craftsmanship in gold, silver, pottery, and woodwork.

Two main influences are apparent in furniture of the Italian Renaissance, and to some extent they were contradictory and difficult to reconcile. The first was the discipline of classical architecture, which began to be studied seriously shortly after 1400. It led to a pedantic insistence on very correct proportions, and the construction of many pieces of furniture as though they were miniature buildings in stone rather than wood. Indeed, various stones, especially coloured marbles, were regularly employed, not only for practical purposes as tops for tables, but also for decorative mosaic work. The wood itself was frequently painted or gilded so that its grain—its 'woodiness'—was concealed—but this had also been true, of course, of much Gothic furniture. And just as the Gothic style had employed such architectural *motifs* as the pointed arch in the construction and decoration of furniture, so the Renaissance used classical columns and entablatures. There is no reason why architecture should not exert this kind of influence on furniture at any given time, provided the designer keeps in mind that it is a piece of furniture he is designing, and not a building.

If the Italian Renaissance sometimes produced pillared cabinets with mosaic doors that look more like temples to the muses (and 'mosaic', in this sense, comes from the Greek word for muse, and has nothing whatever to do with Moses) it also went to the other extreme, allowing sculpture and painting to revolt against architectural discipline and create the kind of extravagances we call Baroque. This was the second of the great influences of the Renaissance. It reached perfection in fifteenth- and sixteenth-century Italy, under Michelangelo and his followers, and spread across Europe to affect profoundly the furnishing styles of all countries. According to national temperament and conditions, it was variously adapted and digested, its effect being more marked, and lasting longer, in some countries than in others.

I think it is true to say that, of all the many factors that went to make up the revolution in thought and practice that is called the Renaissance, so far as the decorative arts are concerned the three most vital were these:

(i) The re-discovery of Greek and Roman ideas of what is good and beautiful in architecture and sculpture.
(ii) The fall of Constantinople and the consequent influx to Rome and the rest of Italy of craftsmen with the skills and traditions of Byzantine culture.

(iii) A spontaneous upsurge of genius that really has little to do with historic cause and effect—for example, Dante's *Inferno* owes little or nothing to the Greek or Latin classic writers.

I am sorry if all this seems terribly academic and out of place in a book expressly written for people who want a bit of antique furniture in a small modern house, but if we are to understand, even dimly, the reasons for furniture being the way it is, some familiarity with the background against which it was made is absolutely essential. A piece of furniture can be chosen for many reasons—because it is pretty, or useful; because it will impress the neighbours; because it fits into a recess or matches the piano or happens to be priced at exactly the amount of the check which Uncle Edwin gave as a wedding present. All these may be perfectly valid reasons for acquiring an antique, but to appreciate what has been bought, the reasons for its manufacture, in the first place, have to be taken into account. And with 'foreign' furniture, especially, there is a strong tendency, at least among the English, to reject what is unfamiliar and difficult to understand.

Consequently, furniture of the Renaissance is rather out of fashion at the present time, except in Italy itself. Italian dealers are scouring Europe for it, and though the price is creeping up now, because of their interest in it, it is still possible to buy it at prices which, considering its superb quality and magnificent decorative possibilities, are ridiculously low. Altogether, I feel it is worth listing a few of the types most frequently encountered —not of Italian origin only, but the French, Spanish and Portuguese, Dutch and English adaptations.

Italy

As in most other countries, the commonest piece of furniture was the chest. We have already discussed, in Chapter Two, the Gothic type of plank construction, and the later variety with panelled construction, developed in Holland and exploited all over northern Europe. In Italy, the chest occupied an even more important place in the household, and according to the means of the owner, so time and money were lavished on its construction and decoration. The *cassone*, to give it the Italian name by which

A.

B.

Fig. 4

The Renaissance in Italy

A. Cabinet-of-drawers on stand, the legs of caryatid form, sixteenth century.

B. *Cassone* of sarcophagus shape, late fifteenth century.

it is known, was usually constructed of walnut or cypress, and carved in high relief, favourite subjects being the family coat-of-arms, foliage, figures representing the Christian saints of the pagan gods and goddesses of mythology, and—as the restless Baroque feeling gained momentum—elaborate scrollwork. In all but the poorest families it was the custom to give the bride a dower chest, and when the *cassone* was serving this purpose, it was often decorated with a painted panel depicting a famous love-story. For the great houses, great artists worked—and not merely as designers. There are *cassoni* existing to this day with paintings executed by such masters as Botticelli and Pietro di Cosimo. Others were covered with a layer of hard plaster called *gesso*, which was intricately carved and then gilded. The shape varied from the rectangular box that had served in Gothic times to a sarcophagus-form that tapered down towards the feet, sometimes in a straight line, sometimes following a curve (Fig. 4).

Visitors to London can see, at the Courtauld Institute, two very fine *cassoni*, set among other splendid Renaissance pieces, not to mention the fine collection of pictures. These are large and ornate examples, little suited to use in the modern home; but smaller and simpler specimens are to be found, which would grace any hall or living-room of good proportions. A *cassone* is a commanding piece of furniture that looks its best against a plain, even severe background, or else against rich and ruddy draperies. I would favour a white wall or a window hung with crimson velvet curtains, but I must confess that mine has to be accommodated under the stairs in a narrow hall, where it does not look its handsome best, but does hold a lot of blankets and bed-linen. The *cassone* is essentially functional, and often did service as a seat when chairs were still scarce. Sometimes it was fitted with a back and arms, and became akin to the settle commonly found in the country districts of Britain, Holland, and America. When the *cassone* is fitted with a back, it is called a *cassa panca*. The Metropolitan Museum of Art in New York boasts an example almost nine feet in length, but again, smaller specimens are to be bought.

I must confess I have never really understood why chairs should have continued to be scarce, even in Italy, birthplace and cradle of the Renaissance, as late as 1600. Some magnificent throne-like constructions were made, which were usually more or less permanent fixtures. A lighter and more portable type of chair was made to fold, having an X-shaped frame, back and front, which closed up like a pair of scissors. This is known in Italy as a *Savonarola*, presumably because it was popular in Florence at about the time the martyred monk was dictator of that city. In Germany, it is also associated with the Reformation, but is given a national flavour by calling it a *Luther* chair. A more correct name, indicating its true origins, is *curule*, which is what the Romans had called the stool of similar shape used by a chief magistrate to sit on when riding in a chariot. Don't let these fancy names concern you too much. Most English writers are content to call this type of chair an 'X' chair. A version of it was current in Britain early in the seventeenth century (see p. 62).

Another portable type of chair in sixteenth-century Italy was the *Sgabello*. This had a tall, narrow back, a solid seat and legs composed either of two solid slabs of wood, one at the front and one at the rear, or three staves thrust into the underside of the seat, milk-maid's-stool fashion. In Britain these are known as 'gossip' or 'spinning' chairs, and are said to have been used by the women while spinning a yarn in more senses than one. This, so far as Britain is concerned, is probably an old wives' tale in itself, or possibly a dealers' story. I doubt very much whether any of these chairs were made in England until some coarse reproductions, with treacly black stain over the crude carving, was turned out in late Victorian times. They are still being made today, and are offered for sale, quite honestly, in the shops specializing in the sort of furniture that no one seems to want to buy if it is genuine. The type is related to the French 'caqueteuse' (see p. 43).

The paucity of chairs throughout Europe at a time when their rather tricky construction had been mastered can only be explained—and then not very satisfactorily—by the persisting social taboo that reserved chairs for important people (it persists to this day in our use of the term 'chairman') and also by an aesthetic objection, very marked in even the largest Italian palaces, to cluttering any room, especially its centre, with an excess of furniture. The magnificence of individual pieces told to good effect only if they could be given reasonable wall space, and could be viewed at a little distance. An arrangement of tables and chairs in the middle of the room, such as we often have today, which tends to make even a nobly proportioned *salôn* take on the air of a village hall set out for a whist drive, would have interfered with the view of the wall-pieces.

These included, as well as the omnipresent *cassone*, various types of cabinet and cupboard. There was the full-length cabinet with solid doors, from which the modern wardrobe is derived, but which had few English counterparts. In Spain, Germany, and France, however, it became a standard item, and as it has come to be thought of as characteristically French, with the French name of *armoire*, we will postpone its consideration for the moment, reviewing more typically Italian pieces in the meantime.

Of these, the architecturally conceived cabinet of drawers is perhaps the piece that is met with most often—and most often overlooked or dismissed as a useless article of furniture that has no place in the modern home. True, the elaborate arrangement of small drawers, set within a carcase and usually mounted on a stand which is really in the form of a table, is limited in its practical application. The drawers were intended to contain small and precious objects, and those of us who have anything of the sort, these days, usually prefer to display them rather than hide them away. And yet there must be many uses for these dignified and pleasing pieces of furniture, when you consider all the bits and pieces that are not fit for display, that get lost in large drawers and cause frayed tempers because they can never be found when wanted—everything from a card of fuse-wire to the football-pool coupons. Anyone with a tidy mind could have a glorious time with one of these cabinets, gathering together all the little homeless objects in a house and allocating a drawer to this and that. Very often there is a small compartment set at the centre, having a miniature 'front door' with its own pillasters and pediment. The stand is usually about two-and-a-half feet high, with two or three elaborate legs at the front, and plainer ones at the back. The way in which the legs are elaborated provides a clue as to date, and in cases of doubt, to nationality, as these cabinets were much imitated in other countries. National varieties will be noted in due course. Early Italian specimens frequently have legs in the form of caryatids—semi-human figures, carved and sometimes gilt. The cabinet on stand can vary in size, the smaller ones being only about three feet across and under six feet in overall height, so that size alone cannot be made a good reason for rejecting them as furnishing pieces in the smaller house. They are among the most obviously under-priced items on the market today (Fig. 4).

In case it should be thought that I am waxing unduly enthusiastic about Italian Renaissance furniture, I would venture a word of warning about a certain type of table of the period which is sometimes bought in the mistaken belief that it will serve the purpose of a dining-table. Like any long narrow table with some carving to it, it is usually described as a 'refectory table'. It normally has a pair of turned legs at each end which rest on a cross-piece. Under the table top is a deep frieze (not deep freeze!) in which drawers are set. The frieze and the drawer-fronts which form part of it are not usually flat and vertical, but curved in cross section, so that the bottom edge recedes, thus creating an illusion that there is more knee-room for anyone sitting at the table than is, in fact, the case. These tables, or *banconi*, were really intended, like so much of the Italian furniture of the time, to be placed against the wall. They are not really meant for sitting at, and can be most uncomfortable as dining-tables. They were reproduced in vast numbers in the nineteenth century, mostly in oak with nasty black stain on it. Genuine Italian pieces of the sixteenth and seventeenth centuries are almost always of walnut, used in the solid and not exhibiting the elaborately figured grain of burr-walnut used as veneers—which is the only kind of walnut many people recognize as such. Solid walnut, as used for this early Italian furniture, is very like that employed for the stocks of good sporting guns. Study that, and you will know how to recognize it.

It was not, of course, the only wood used. I have made mention of cypress. This, and pine, were employed with a coating of *gesso* for the pieces intended to be painted or gilt. (The term 'pine' is used, as in most books about old furniture, as a generic one to cover a number of coniferous timbers that includes all varieties of the pine-tree itself, together with fir and larch.) When decoration took the form of inlaying a design, woods of contrasting colours were used, such as fruitwoods—pear and citrus—acacia and sycamore. Other materials used for inlay were ivory, bone, shell, coloured stones, silver, and pewter. When these metals were employed, they were usually engraved.

The softer woods such as pine and lime were much favoured for the very elaborate carving of frames for pictures and mirrors. Until the middle of the seventeenth century, Italy—to be precise, Venice—had a virtual monopoly in the manufacture of mirror-glass. Better and larger pieces of glass were made here than anywhere else in the world, and the secret of their manufacture was jealously guarded, the workmen being forbidden, on pain of death, to reveal it. A looking-glass was thus a valuable object, and no expense was considered too great in preparing a frame for it.

Italian frames dating from the late sixteenth century onwards demonstrate the transition from disciplined Renaissance to extravagant, High Baroque as nothing else can. Plate II provides a good example. It shows a carved pine frame of seventeenth-century Italian workmanship—most probably Florentine. There is not a straight line to be seen in it anywhere, whereas the carcase of the cabinét-on-stand shown in Fig. 4 is essentially rectilinear. Not all examples of the Baroque are quite so curving and curling as is this mirror-frame—not everything offers such opportunities for reckless abandon; but the principal features here are characteristic of the style as a whole. Notice that the curves—excluding the internal oval—do not become a continuous flow, but turn in on themselves to form scrolls, or else come to abrupt stops. They are mostly S-shaped rather than C-shaped, and some of them have an almost savage, hook-like appearance that accords well enough with the grotesque sea-monsters and satyr-masks, but hardly with the musicianly cherubim or—keeping to the Italian idiom—*putti*. The swags of fruit and the overhanging shell are also typical Baroque *motifs*. Considering the thing as a whole, it will be noticed that, in spite of its fantastic elaboration, the design is almost perfectly symmetrical. This point is an important one to keep in mind when we come to examine the transition from Baroque to Rococo, in the next chapter.

It must be borne in mind that the Italians themselves designate the centuries differently. What we call, in English, the 'sixteenth century' (1500–1600) is, in Italian, the 'cinqecento'—the 'fifteenth century'.

In writing of Italian furniture, I have made no attempt to designate the succeeding periods by any particular names, such as those of kings and princes, as the history of the country and its division into small states can really only be sorted out by a keen student of Italian affairs during the Renaissance. Personally, I have never got much further than the romantic but confused picture of the times presented by such names as Medici, Borgia, Machiavelli, with a scheming pope or two thrown in for good measure. In this I think I am probably no more and no less enlightened than are most British people. However, the near-impossibility of labelling Italian periods neatly, according to the name of this or that petty tyrant, should be no bar to the study and appreciation of the furniture itself. It has its place in the modern home, if we care to move the sideboard and adjust our ideas to accommodate it. For those wishing to go more deeply into the subject, detailed classification is best made according to cities—Florence, Venice, Rome, and so on.

France

Because France was a more united country at an earlier date, and because many of its kings—not to mention their queens and mistresses—took a keen interest in the art of furnishing and décor, it is not only possible but right and proper to classify its furniture according to the names of the more important rulers. The less important ones are usually left out of the picture, the periods of furniture being conveniently listed under a few well-known names, with the word 'style' preceding them.

Thus we have 'Style Louis XII' which also covers the reign of his predecessor, Charles VIII, and again, 'Style Henry II' which takes in those of the next three kings as well. So if you did French history for that Honours Degree you nearly didn't get, and if you still retain any of it, don't think I haven't done my homework if I cheerfully ignore the existence of two-thirds of the French monarchy. Here we go with the first batch. If you are English or American, and seeking a reputation among your friends as an expert on antique furniture—learn them off by heart. No one else has ever heard of anyone but Louis XIV, Louis XV and Louis XVI, and most people have difficulty in discriminating between them when it comes to furniture.

Louis XII (Early sixteenth century). Still essentially Gothic, but feeling the effects of the Renaissance as a result of an unsuccessful French invasion of Italy. The furniture is austere, mostly oak, carefully carved with precise, almost minute detail. You won't find much, outside museums, but it does demonstrate the interesting point that, in time past, war had its consoling features. Armies venturing abroad took home with them something besides the more unmentionable diseases. Even last time, some of the boys returned with good German cameras and passable Persian rugs. The French brought something rather better out of Italy in the early 1500's. They brought the Renaissance—and they didn't even have any cigarettes or gum to trade for it.

Francis I (Mid-sixteenth century). During this reign, the French thoroughly absorbed these ideas from the plains of Lombardy, and the furniture that resulted, though traditional in form, exhibits a feeling of delicacy which very little work executed north of the Alps had formerly displayed. The rather flat carving of the Gothic style gave way to a much more detailed treatment in depth. The cabinet with doors on a columnar stand began to take the place of the cruder hutch. The use of inlay, both of contrasting woods and coloured marble, was increasingly used for decoration. A favourite motif, that was to be exploited for some years to come, not only for furniture but for wall-panelling and the like, was the *cartouche* (Fig. 5), carved, painted or inlaid.

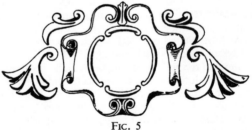

Fig. 5

Cartouche

This kind of motif is an important element in carved decoration from the late sixteenth century onwards, especially on Italian, French and German furniture.

Henry II (mid-to-late sixteenth century). Corresponds roughly to the Elizabethan period in Britain, but shows itself more advanced in its acceptance of Renaissance development. Pre-occupation with the architecture of Ancient Rome is marked, often to a fault, more concern being felt for dignity than for charm. Some of the heavier pieces, such as the *armoire*, take on positively monumental proportions. The example illustrated (Fig. 6) shows the persistence of the Gothic arch in a design of moulded Baroque decoration, and demonstrates the slow process of change. The armoire is a form for which I have great respect —even affection. I always champion its cause, if only to defy the hilarious and irreverent comments of family and friends, provoked by two examples in my own bedroom at home.

FIG. 6

French Provincial *Armoire*, seventeenth century

Though belonging to the Baroque Period, this piece demonstrates the way in which Gothic elements were perpetuated, especially in country-made pieces, well into the seventeenth century.

Admittedly, the larger of the two is a biggish article, but I resent the suggestion that, if I were to install electric lighting, I could make a good thing out of letting it furnished. One source of amusement is the modern ball-castors on which I have mounted it; without them, it requires four strong men to move it when empty; with them, it does rather look as though Emmet had designed it for a *Punch* cover. But it makes a wonderfully commodious wardrobe, with full hanging-length for those long evening-dresses that my wife, perversely, happens not to own, and the fact that she has to stand on a stool to reach the hat-shelf is, after all, a small inconvenience to a woman who seldom wears a hat. When all the jokes have been cracked about it, it's a thumping good piece of furniture that takes up no more room than would a built-in wardrobe, and it cost far less money than is usually spent on such a fitment. I can take it with me if ever I move house—provided I get a gang of workmen to take out the window frames; it won't go through the door.

Henry IV (late sixteenth to early seventeenth century). Chiefly remarkable for the beginnings, in France, of the curving lines of the Baroque, and for an act of religious clemency, the Edict of Nantes, which Henry granted in 1598 to his Protestant subjects. This is an important development which had a strong influence on Dutch and English, and ultimately American, furniture, later in the century. (See p. 49.)

Louis XIII (early to mid-seventeenth century) saw the gradual working-up of French Baroque into an elaboration of heavy, architectural forms with excessive decoration. The whole effect is often depressing, and the untutored observer might well be forgiven, when faced with one of the more extreme examples, for thinking it to be a Victorian monstrosity made for some mill-owner's mansion, about a hundred years ago. This is because Victorian mill-owners had a taste for this sort of thing, and a great deal of heavily carved oak and walnut was manufactured in the nineteenth century to meet their requirements. These pieces were seldom exact copies, authentic 'source-material', as the archivists call it, being relatively scarce in England. The copyists worked from photographs, sketches, memory, and imagination, and there is no doubt that they succeeded in out-Baroquing the Baroque, which was something of a feat. Genuine or bogus, the more massive pieces of this '*Style Louis XIII*' have no place in the smaller house; but there is a danger of becoming completely prejudiced against the period as a whole. Some of the smaller items, especially the gossip-chair—*cacqueteuse*—with its stiffly rounded back, and the dole-cupboard with doors composed of rows of turned members, providing ventilation for foodstuffs —such items as these can often provide that touch of slightly mad extravagance that the otherwise too sober room demands. Continental pieces of this kind blend happily enough with the rather simpler English furniture of the early-seventeenth century, and relieve it of the angular appearance it often has when too much of it is used together.

Louis XIV (mid-seventeenth to early-eighteenth centuries). We are now, I take it, getting on to more familiar ground, and it is probably unnecessary to point out that, coming to the throne in 1643, when he was five years old, and staying there for a solid seventy-two years until he died in 1715, the Grand Monarch set up an unbroken European record for throne-sitting. Seventy-two years may not sound a very long time, set against the whole pattern of history; but when it is kept in mind that, during the same period, Britain fought a protracted civil war, executed Charles I, endured Cromwell and his son, restored the monarchy to Charles II, kicked out James II, invited William of Orange to share the throne with his wife Mary, got Blenheim Palace built under Queen Anne and finally settled for the House of Hanover, with King George upon the Throne—when one digests the fact that all this happened while one king ruled France as an auto-crat, then the weight and force of those seventy-two years begin to tell.

On the arts and crafts they told very heavily indeed, not least on those involving the creation of fine furniture. *Style Louis Quatorze* may not be everyone's cup of tea, but it had a profound effect on design and technique all over Europe and over a long period, and it is only too easy to forget that even the things made in conscious reaction to a particular style owe their existence, in a perverse sort of way, *to* that style. At worst, Louis XIV was a style powerful enough to make it worth while to rebel against it, and before you can understand the results of a rebellion, you must know something of the tyranny that provoked it.

A tyranny of a kind it certainly was. The earlier years of the reign were, so far as furniture was concerned, a hangover from the previous one—Baroque gone mad—but as soon as the young king was old enough to exert an influence, it made itself felt in a return to classical discipline, and the more fantastic elements of the Baroque were licked firmly into shape, without one whit of its essential grandeur being sacrificed. After the death of Mazarin, who had administered the affairs of France while the king was still a child, Louis established himself as an absolute monarch, ruling the country and quarrelling with the rest of Europe from his magnificent headquarters at Versailles. The previous king had used it as a hunting lodge. Louis XIV made it the most splendid palace in Europe. In all this, as in every department of State, he was advised and assisted by his controller-general, Colbert, who appointed the painter Charles Le Brun as virtual dictator of the arts.

These two founded the Academy of Painting and Sculpture, and also a school of industrial art, which was really a splendid furniture-factory, at Gobelins. Today, we think of it mainly as a centre of tapestry-weaving, but in fact it produced most of the furniture—and there was a great deal of it—for the use of the king at Versailles.

Le Brun may be regarded as the presiding genius of the period, exploiting the talents of hundreds of skilled craftsmen to satisfy the megalomania of the king. Of these, the best known maker of furniture is André Charles Buhl (or Boulle), who perfected a method of overlaying wooden surfaces with a veneer of tortoiseshell, dyed red and intricately inlaid with brass. So skilfully was this work executed that virtually no waste was involved. It

Fig. 7

Boulle and Contreboulle

The black area represents stained tortoiseshell, and the clear area, brass. The piece of tortoiseshell cut out for the inlaying of the brass motif is itself used as a motif in a brass ground—often on a different article of furniture. Elaborate patterns are thus built up with the minimum of waste.

resulted in two compositions, identical but for the fact that one was composed of brass inlay on a tortoiseshell ground, and the other of tortoiseshell inlay on a brass ground. The first is called Boulle, the second, counter-Boulle (or, in France, *contreboulle*). It was thus possible to make up pairs of tables and cabinets exhibiting this subtle difference. *Contreboulle* pieces are regarded by some judges to be inferior to *Boulle* but the two results ought to be seen as complementary to each other. (Fig. 7.)

Metal-work played a further part in forming protective mouldings and corner-pieces of gilded bronze, which came to be known as '*ormolu*' mounts. In the reign of Louis XIV, their use was restricted to this protective role, and though they were cast with great attention to detail, it was not until the following century that, as we shall see, ormolu assumed a much greater importance in the enrichment of furniture (see pp. 86, 90).

Wood itself was often carved and gilded so heavily that it has almost the appearance of metal. This is especially true of the splendid stands made to support cabinets of oriental lacquer, brought to Europe by the East India companies from China and Japan. In form, they followed the Italian pattern. More will be said of them when we consider their English usage in the reign of Charles II, but it is important to remember their popularity in France at a slightly earlier date, and the very strong influence that oriental art—not to mention European misconceptions of its real nature—had on Western culture in the seventeenth century.

It was at this time, too, that veneering in fine woods over a carcase of more common timber was extensively used for the first time since the arts of ancient Rome had dwindled and all but died. Veneering is by no means a modern process for jazzing up the glossy walnut bedroom-suites sold by the hire-purchase establishments in the High Street, but an honourable technique for beautifying furniture. It involves cutting carefully selected woods with finely figured grain into thin sheets, and laying them down with glue on to a solid surface. Extensions of the use of veneer are many, but the most important is the matching of veneers to form a symmetrical pattern. Thin slices taken from the same piece of wood will, obviously, all exhibit the same characteristics, and by turning them over, twisting them round, and so on, it is possible to make up a design that is perfectly balanced.

When four pieces of veneer are used in this way, the result is called 'quartered veneers'. A glance at Fig. 8 should make this clear.

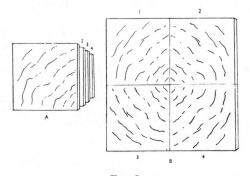

FIG. 8

Building up a pattern with Veneers
The four slices of wood cut from the same piece of timber (A) all have the same grain. By turning them this way and that, they are used to make up a symmetrical pattern, (B).

Such a technique has strict limitations if it is employed with solid timber. Not only is it impossible to get many pieces of great thickness with matching grain, but the practical difficulties of setting them together, edge-to-edge, are very considerable. They need to be set up as a panel within a frame, which makes flush surfaces out of the question, and they are very prone to warps and cracks. Elaborately figured woods lack the stability of straight-grained timbers, and are thus inclined to crack for the very reason—the curl in the grain—that makes them beautiful. By cutting them into thin veneers and mounting them on to a suitable foundation, these difficulties are largely overcome.

A further use of veneers was the inlaying of one into another to form a pictorial design. This technique is called *marquetry*. A further refinement was to band flat surfaces with a narrow border of veneer, usually with a prominently marked straight grain that ran at right-angles to the edge of the piece. This is known as 'cross-banding', and it was much exploited, not only in France, but in Holland and Britain too, at a rather later date, as we shall see when we come to consider Dutch and English furniture. The inner edge of the cross-band was usually divided from the main surface-area by a thin line of contrasting veneer, known as stringing'. For dark stringing, ebony was used extensively, and for light, almost white lines, box-wood. The principal veneers used by the French in the seventeenth century were burr-walnut, laburnum, and ebony. It was this last-named wood that first gave to the skilled worker his title of *ébéniste*, the carpenter who assembled the solid foundation being called a *menuisier*.

This division of labour into grades began under Louis XIV and became more marked as the seventeenth century advanced and greater elaboration called for more and more specialization. For example, while surfaces such as table-tops and drawer-fronts, doors and end-panels were frequently decorated with marquetry, the legs of the same pieces might also be richly carved. Originally, the *menuisier* was entrusted with this work, but for the finest pieces, the skill of the carpenter was insufficient, and the craft of the carver emerged as a separate trade.

These craftsmen formed their separate guilds. From the outset the standard of entry was high, as befitted a trade catering for an exacting monarch who dictated taste to a nobility he did much to make effete and powerless. This autocracy of taste, worked out by Le Brun and his team of designers, decided very largely what furniture should be made for the king and court, and also for a flourishing bourgeoisie who aped the nobility, in ways that Molière satirized in *Le Bourgeois Gentilhomme*. (This play was written expressly for the entertainment of Louis and his court, with whom it was a great success. Apropos of the taste for things oriental, it is worth noting that the hilarious climax of the comedy turns on some of the characters dressing themselves up as Turks—a charade suggested to the playwright by the king himself. The point here is that European notions of the geography of the East were, in the seventeenth century, so vague that words like 'Chinese', 'Japanese', 'Indian', and 'Turkish' were used more or less indiscriminately, and Louis would probably have been quite happy if the 'Turks' had appeared dressed as mandarins or rajahs. What Europe expected of the Orient was a sublime hotch-potch of exotic fantasy.)

There was many a *bourgeois gentilhomme* about at the time,

for Colbert, himself of middle-class stock, saw to it that most of the real work of government was done by people drawn from the same sort of background as his own, while the aristocrats were fobbed off with sinecures entailing nothing more nor less exacting than a punctilious attendance at court. The middle-class thus grew rich and powerful, and equipped their homes with furniture by the lesser craftsmen of Paris that imitated, as far as means would permit, the royal creations of Gobelins. Much of this furniture is in really shocking taste, being monumental yet not magnificent, and ornate without the saving grace that is provided only by the hidden but firmly restraining influence of a master-designer. I have written (p. 42) that the Victorians 'succeeded in out-Baroquing the Baroque'. It is equally true to say that the seventeenth-century bourgeoisie largely succeeded in anticipating the Victorians.

As for the working-folk, they were exploited by their employers and found no champion in the king, who hated and feared them. They had a hard struggle to keep alive, and what little furniture they owned was of the crudest kind.

To find simple furniture of the period, one must look rather to the provinces and the country districts, where substantial pieces of traditional type were made, echoing only quietly the loud voices of Paris and Versailles. Of these provincial centres, Lyons was one of the more important, producing very good, honest and even elaborate pieces. French provincial furniture of the seventeenth and eighteenth centuries is now deservedly fashionable, the fine chests-of-drawers, made so well of solid oak, fruitwood or walnut, usually being described by the dealers who specialize in them as 'commodes' but, strictly speaking, this term should be reserved for the more sophisticated examples made in the capital.

The chest-of-drawers was a piece of furniture that developed early in the seventeenth century from the time-honoured, box-type chest, which is really the father and mother of most of the furniture used for storage of clothes and valuables. A transitional form is the mule-chest, which is of box-construction, but has a long drawer, often disguised with applied mouldings to make it look like two. The drawer was at first a novelty and a luxury, and it was natural enough, if you could afford only one, to shoot a line by pretending you could rise to two. Gradually, all over

Europe, the box-construction gave way to drawer-accommodation, until the old oak chest of Britain and Holland, the *cassone* of Italy, the *coffre* or *caisse* of France, had become either a chest-of-drawers, plain and simple, or a commode of elaborate design. (See Fig. 9.) In the second half of the century, many chests were mounted on stands of varying heights, but in the main, this trend was more marked in Holland and Britain than in France, and a description of the type will be found on p. 79.

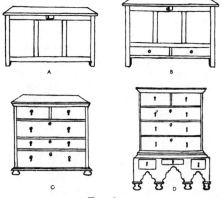

Fig. 9
Evolution of the Chest
A. Box-type chest or 'coffer', circa 1600.
B. Mule-chest, circa 1625.
C. Chest-of-drawers, circa 1675.
D. Chest-on-stand or 'low-boy', circa 1690.

Both these countries were to benefit as a direct result of an inept act of intolerance on the part of the French king, when, in 1685, he revoked the Edict of Nantes (see p. 42) and thus terrified thousands of French Protestants into fleeing the country. Many of these Huguenots sought refuge in England and Holland, where they were made welcome. The Republic of Holland had no love of the Grand Monarch, and had in fact been waging sporadic war against him until only a few years before. As for the British, they had good commercial, as well as religious, grounds for taking in these homeless people, most of whom were highly skilled craftsmen. In twenty years, from 1670 to 1690, over 75,000 French textile-workers became naturalized British subjects, and their skill rapidly laid the foundations of a valuable industry which the government was not slow to subsidize and protect.

One of the designers and craftsmen who fled France at this time, to make his home in Holland, was Daniel Marot. He rose to be cabinet-maker-in-chief to William of Orange, who shortly after became King of England, ruling jointly with his English wife Mary. From this example alone, it can easily be appreciated how the furniture of one country becomes influenced by that of another, even by the enforcement into exile of one individual.

Marot is traditionally credited with developing legs for tables and chairs following the S-shaped curve of the Baroque. It is not clear what grounds there are for accepting this, as the shape had certainly been employed in Italy, early in the seventeenth century. True, it never became popular in France until the latter part of the century, the classical discipline of the Le Brun school insisting, for the most part, on a vertical leg, tapering slightly, with a swelling about two-thirds or three-quarters the way up. Both types of leg—vertical and semi-scroll—seem to have been popular in Holland from about 1680 to 1700. The scroll-leg is, it seems to me, much more likely to have been introduced into Holland before Marot's time, and grafted on to traditional forms—as were so many other Baroque features—as the result of the long occupation by Spain of the Netherlands. (See Fig 14E.)

Spain

Spain herself had been, for centuries, a half-eastern country, the greater part of the peninsula being under Moorish rule.

The last of the Moorish rulers in Spain was expelled before the end of the fifteenth century, at a time roughly coinciding with the beginning of the Renaissance in Italy. On the one hand, there were fairly strong contacts between Spain and Italy, so that Renaissance ideas penetrated Spanish thought, and Spanish furniture of the sixteenth and seventeenth centuries exhibits Italian influence in a marked way. At the same time, the Moorish tradition remained very much alive, because, although their domination was broken, the Moors did not leave the country to a man, and many who remained were fine craftsmen. The result was a hybrid style, half-Moorish, half-European, which is called *Mudejar*.

A good example of the combination of Spanish, Moorish and Italian ideas is to be found in an article of furniture called a *vargueño* or *bargueño*—from Vargas or Bargas, the town where it was reputed to have first been made. This is really our old friend, the cabinet-on-stand, which we have met before and shall certainly meet again; in this Spanish version, the cabinet has the usual interior fitment of drawers, but instead of being enclosed with doors, there is a fall-front hinged on the bottom edge, so that it falls forward to form a writing-desk. The interior drawers are usually richly decorated, either with gilding, carving, or ivory inlay—often a combination of all three. In this it differs little from its Italian counterpart. The truly Spanish-Moorish flavour is often provided by an exterior covered with velvet or finely tooled and painted Cordoban leather, over which are laid beautifully wrought mounts of iron—a craft in which the Spaniards have always excelled. Quite often, the legs of the stand are braced with wrought iron struts. A variation is the *papelera*, a *vargueño* with no fall-front, and fitted with small feet (see Plate III), which also rests on a stand braced with iron.

This bracing with ironwork is a characteristic Spanish technique. Also typical is the fondness for splaying table-legs at an angle—the sort of angle we find in the legs of a milk-maid's stool or, for that matter, in a vast amount of contemporary furniture of the kind that looks as though it is doing the splits. Spanish tables of the sixteenth and seventeenth centuries attempt the same gymnastic feat with rather more success.

This is not always the case with Spanish essays in the Baroque manner, which frequently reached a degree of extravagance that is positively alarming. In Italy, the bold curves of the Baroque had largely been confined to decorating pieces of furniture which were otherwise of rectilinear structure; exceptions to this rule were to be found in some chairs of very ornate design produced in Venice and Florence. These extreme models were to provide the dubious inspiration for some extraordinary Spanish chairs, made in the early seventeenth century, where the avowed intention seems to have been the avoidance of any straight line whatsoever. Back, seat, legs, and arms are one fantastic tangle of gilded and painted scrolls, often entwined with foliage and with four or five little naked cherubs swarming over the framework. That is fair enough—these chairs are eminently suited for small boys to practise their tree-climbing at an early age.

Obviously, such extravaganzas as these are hardly suitable for use in a small modern home, but one of the functions of a book like this is to suggest what should be avoided, as well as advising on what should be acquired. However, even Spanish Baroque at its inebriated climax can provide the occasional article of value in furnishing a modern interior. Though normally on a scale to suit one of Hollywood's larger and more ego-centric film-producers, these chairs were sometimes made in miniature, and a child-size effort really is an irresistible bit of nonsense that can look quite wonderful in a fairly small and otherwise austere room.

Another adaptable item of Spanish baroquerie is the bench or form, about five feet in length, with an elaborately carved back. It is possible, without doing any damage to the article, to use it as the head of a bed, resting one end of a divan-bed on the seat, and supporting the other end on a simple wooden structure made to size. I once saw this done very simply indeed—the foot of the bed rested, very securely, on a couple of beer crates, which normally were hidden by the bed-spread. The back of the form, richly carved, made a splendid-looking headboard, and if it proved a bit uncomfortable when the occupant was sitting up in bed drinking her morning tea, no doubt she felt this was more than compensated for by the faint but unmistakable note of voluptuousness it lent to her bachelor flat. A maiden lady of unimpeachable character, she had a fondness for domestic touches that might have come naturally to someone like Lucrezia Borgia, and did much to console her in a rather lonely life made up of good works and public transport. There is something to be said, after all, for furnishing your home as a background, not for the kind of person you are obliged to be, but for the sort of character you secretly admire and would like to emulate. Foolish and impractical? Of course. Why not? And if you want to know how I came to find out about the beer crates, I feel no shame in admitting that I crawled under the bed in the interests of pure research.

Such exotic items as baroque bed-heads are by no means all that Spain has to offer, in furniture of the earlier periods, that is of interest to the modern home-maker. Simple, country-made pieces, such as long narrow tables with slightly splayed legs braced with wrought iron supports, can be very useful indeed, often being lighter in construction and smaller in size than the English equivalent, the so-called 'refectory' table. Wrought-iron strap-work, locks and hinges enrich attractive and useful cupboards of varying sizes, and there are some good small ones to be found, of the type we call a 'hutch', that blend equally well with cottage or more sophisticated furniture. True, they are not plentiful outside Spain, except in countries influenced by Spanish conquest, but they do sometimes crop up for sale in unexpected places, and because they are 'foreign' and 'strange', they are often sold for far less than a more orthodox, native equivalent will bring.

The ability to recognize such pieces for what they are, coupled with sufficient imagination to exploit their possibilities, can pay handsome dividends in these days when so many people are avidly chasing the fashionable, elegant and conventional items that we shall come to consider in the chapter 'Rococo to Neo-Classic'.

Portugal

Portuguese furniture, though in many ways similar to Spanish, has certain unique things to offer that are of considerable interest in this respect.

In the main, the furniture of Portugal is much less influenced by Moorish elements in design, but more than makes up for this by the consequences of contacts further east. The Portuguese were among the first to trade with China, India, and the East Indies. This becomes very evident when we come, inevitably, to look at one of our standard examples, the cabinet-on-stand, and the form it took in seventeenth-century Portugal. Not only do we find the usual Chinese and Japanese lacquer cabinets, but also a very curious variety actually made in the Portuguese settlement in Goa, India (Plate IV). The wood is usually a variety of red wood, with ebony mouldings and an elaborate design inlaid with bone. The legs were carved by the Indians into semi-human shapes, usually mermaids, mermen, or native deities. Frankly, they are not 'beautiful' to Western eyes brought up to appreciate the Hellenistic concept, but they have an undeniable power and fascination. Such pieces are by no means commonplace, nor are they cheap when being offered for sale by a dealer who under-stands just what he has for sale, as there are serious collectors of Indo-Portuguese furniture who are willing to pay for its interest, quality and rarity. But the dealer who would understand such a piece is almost as rare as the article itself, and there is always a chance of finding one at a bargain price in an otherwise expensive shop.

Another reason for noting this East Indies work is its influence on Dutch and English cabinet-work of the late seventeenth century. This Portuguese-English contact was made direct by the marriage of Charles II to Katherine of Braganza, and there is even a scrolled foot, introduced into Britain at that time, still known as a 'Braganza foot'. (See Fig. 12B.)

Portuguese influence on Dutch work was less direct, coming as a result of the rivalry between the Dutch and Portuguese East India Companies—trade rivalry always stimulating the noble art of imitation—and also via Spain. As Spain and Portugal share a long frontier, it is only natural that the ideas of the one country should have a marked influence on those of the other, and since the Netherlands and Portugal were for so long under Spanish rule, inevitably Dutch design was modified by Portuguese as well as Spanish feeling.

The Netherlands

We have already noted (p. 24) that it was in the Low Countries that framed construction for chests and tables was developed in the mid-sixteenth century. There was a powerful tradition of native craftsmanship in the Netherlands, dating back to the Middle Ages. Belgium did not exist as an independent state until the early nineteenth century, and what is now Belgium and Holland was divided, at the end of the sixteenth century and for long after, into the Northern and Southern Netherlands. The northern provinces were Protestant, and the southern—known as the Spanish Netherlands—were Catholic. (All this history, geography and religion may seem of little account to the modern man or woman looking for a table or chair to put in the spare bedroom, but these are the factors that decided the form that the table or chair should take.) The net outcome of this confused, war-ridden period of Dutch and Flemish history is that furniture made in the Spanish, or Southern, Netherlands shows much more

Spanish influence than that made in the United Provinces in the north.

This means, in practice, a more florid style, with greater use of carving, and a readier acceptance of the Baroque, in the southern work. In the north, at least until the middle of the seventeenth century, carving was restrained, and decoration was provided by the use of rather heavy mouldings arranged geometrically and applied to the surface of doors and drawer-fronts with pins and glue. On the best quality furniture of the first half of the seventeenth century, these mouldings were carved out of the solid. A very similar style of decoration was currently fashionable in Britain, where we know it by the name of 'Jacobean' (see pp. 59, 63). Dutch mouldings, however, were rather heavier than the English.

A characteristic Dutch article of this simple, solid sort is the cupboard illustrated in Fig. 10. The doors are 'fielded'—that is

FIG. 10

Seventeenth-century Dutch *Kas* with Moulded Decoration
This type, like many other traditional European articles of furniture, was also made by Early Settlers in America.

to say, the panels are bevelled on the face side, exploiting bevelling as a decorative feature, and not merely as a practical device for making the edges of the panel thinner for fitting into the frame-work. (When this is the sole consideration, the panel is roughly bevelled on the reverse side.) Further decoration is provided by applied lozenges and split prisms. This article is known as a *kas*, and is typical not only of mid-seventeenth native Dutch work, but also of that made by emigrants from Holland to America.

Dutch influence on early American furniture was doubly strong because of direct emigration and also, indirectly, the powerful impact on English styles that came about when William of Orange became King of England (see p. 77 *et. seq.*).

As with the furniture of most countries, a distinction has to be drawn between the simpler styles made in the country towns and the more elaborate items devised to furnish the homes of noblemen and rich merchants. In spite of powerful democratic traditions, this is as true of Holland as of any other country.

Of the less pretentious pieces, one of the most popular in Holland over a very long period was the dresser. Originally, this article of furniture was simply a side-board with drawers and, sometimes, cupboards below, intended mainly for the display of whatever silver plate—or failing silver, then pewter—the proud householder could boast. In the seventeenth century, however, the Dutch East India Company brought blue-and-white porcelain home from China, and it became so popular that the little town of Delft, famous for its beer, went over from brewing to pottery as its chief industry. These Delft wares had somehow to be accommodated, and the furniture makers produced wall-racks —still known as Delft-racks—for the purpose. The next step was to attach them to the top of the dresser as a super-structure. The same story is true of English dressers. The Dutch type usually has cupboards below and often small ones above, set at the ends of the shelves. This was imitated in English North Country versions (see p. 160). A feature found in the Dutch variety only is a domed, or rounded, top to the rack of shelves.

The 'Eighty Years War' against Spanish tyranny ended with victory for Holland in 1648, and the second half of the century, though far from trouble-free, saw a growing improvement in the country's fortunes and a consequent demand for finer furniture to meet the needs of a flourishing merchant class. Techniques were developed and acquired by native ingenuity and also from the influx of French Protestant craftsmen escaping religious persecution.

Notably, the use of solid oak gave way to veneering in walnut, both plain and with marquetry decoration. The Dutch were especially fond of a rather florid style of marquetry, involving bold designs of flowers, foliage and birds. A more compact style followed a little later, composed of an all-over pattern of small and precise scrolls, or arabesques, known as 'seaweed' marquetry. Both types persisted for a very long time, in Holland.

Britain

Late Elizabethan. In the year 1600, the ageing queen still occupied her throne, more securely than ever before. Her enemies, at home and abroad, were either utterly defeated or reduced to ineffective conspiracy. It was, for the English, a time of material prosperity, and their society was, in many ways, more authentically affluent than is our own today. A middle-class of merchants and small land-owners was steadily increasing both its numbers and its power, and the direct result was the building and furnishing of many houses.

Most furniture was constructed of native oak, elm and ash, sometimes inlaid with fruitwoods, sycamore, and holly. Elm and ash are frequently mistaken for oak, but in general, their grain is more open. Large pieces of elm were commonly used for the seats of chairs, and for carcase furniture and table-tops too, but it is so prone to attacks by wood-worm that much early furniture made of it has not survived. Ash was also used in boards, as a substitute for oak, and because of its suppleness, in thin sections for bending into curves. (See the reference to Windsor chairs, in the Chapter on Rural Traditions, p. 164.) Beech, birch and, indeed, any native woods were employed, as adjuncts to, or as substitutes for, the tough, long lasting oak.

Timber from orchards—apple and pear—has been utilized for a great deal of country-made furniture for centuries, both in Britain and on the Continent. Holly, being the whitest wood available in Britain, has always been a favourite for inlaying, especially where narrow, distinct lines in contrast to the darker ground are required.

Elizabeth is credited with causing walnut trees to be planted on a fairly large scale. Although they are said to have been brought here by the Romans, there were relatively few in Britain before the seventeenth century, and those planted on Elizabeth's instructions did not reach maturity for more than half a century; though a few pieces of English manufacture have come down to us—just to make life difficult for writers who want to generalize—it is true to say that most walnut furniture of the late sixteenth and early seventeenth centuries found in Great Britain can be traced to a continental origin. Visitors to that remarkable Elizabethan mansion in Somerset, Montacute House, may recall a 'refectory' table and two Savonarola chairs made of walnut, all of them sixteenth-century Italian workmanship. In fact they are not part of the original furnishings. If they were, we could get out of it very neatly by stressing that, certainly from the time of Henry VIII, furniture was imported into Britain, particularly from Italy and the Low Countries, on a fairly large scale.

We have already noted (pp. 26, 27) that the extending dining-table was first imported from Flanders and then imitated here. Stools and the longer edition of them—benches or forms—long continued to be the principal kind of seating at the table, under which they were stowed when not in use. The old Gothic type with shaped supports acting as legs (see p. 21) gradually gave way to framed construction in the Flemish manner, the legs being turned on the lathe in a variety of baluster shapes, a square being left top and bottom into which rails were mortised and tenoned, the joint being secured with wooden dowel-pins (see Fig. 11), the ends of which can always be seen. The top was also fixed by dowel-pins driven through *into the edge of the rails*. Pins which have been driven through the top and *into the leg* are, usually, not original. This does not necessarily mean that the stool is not genuine, as the top sometimes warped and the unsecured corners, over the legs, were inclined to rise, in which case dowel-pins may have been driven through at these points to correct the warp. Quite often, however, pins at these corner positions indicate that the top has, at some time, been replaced or completely renewed—and by an amateur, at that. An experienced craftsman would hesitate to drive a dowel-pin downwards into the end grain of the leg, as to do so is to run a grave risk of splitting it.

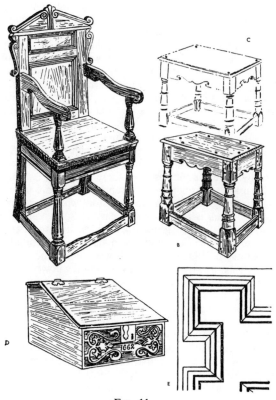

FIG. 11

English Oak of the Late Tudor and Early Stuart Periods

A. Arm-chair, late-sixteenth to early-seventeenth centuries.
B. 'Joyned' stool, early- to mid-seventeenth century, showing correct positions for dowel-pins.
C. 'Joyned' stool, showing incorrect positions for dowel-pins.
D. Bible-box, early seventeenth century type persisting to 1700 and even later.
E. Detail of geometrically arranged mouldings for drawer-fronts, early-seventeenth century.

Provided the top is an old one, the fact that it was replaced —perhaps a couple of hundred years ago—is insufficient reason for rejecting it, and indeed this may seem a footling point to make at all. The reason I do so is that these joint-stools or 'coffin' stools, as they are popularly known ('joyned' was the original word) are now very much sought after. They serve very well as coffee-tables and bedside-tables in the modern home, being the right height for use with present-day chairs, settees and divan-beds, which used to be so much higher that tables were seldom less than 2 ft. 4 in. in height. This means that a genuinely antique 'coffee-table' is a very difficult thing to find, there being, in practice, only the little Georgian tripod wine-table, the Sheraton nest of spindly-legged tables and the old oak joyned stool itself that really serve the purpose. All these are being reproduced in their thousands. Straightforward reproductions are usually easy enough to recognize, but the joyned stool which has been made up from old oak is not always so easy to spot. Various points need to be checked. In genuine examples, the stretchers below always exhibit signs of wear from having had countless feet resting on them. (When these stools were in use, the main hall of the house was strewn with rushes which were allowed to accumulate like deep litter in a hen-house. They stank to high heaven unless regularly sprinkled with aromatic herbs, and the filth underfoot must have been appalling. Anyone who really wants to keep his Tudor or Stuart house strictly in period will perhaps appreciate my doubts expressed in the Introduction. The point here is that it was the most natural thing in the world to hitch your feet over the under-rails of stools to get them out of the muck, not to mention the draught, for a little while, and those rails ought to bear witness to the fact. Good fakers are aware of this, and carefully simulate the effect with the aid of a spoke-shave. A little experience will soon enable the amateur to spot tool-marks where only those of boots should be apparent. The general principle is one that can be applied over a very wide range of old furniture indeed.) Because the demand comfortably exceeds the supply, sixteen pounds and upwards is regularly charged for joyned stools. Few dealers, even, know the secret of deciding whether the top has been disturbed or not, by the position of the pins, so the buyer really does need to know, for himself, how to assess the degree of authenticity and the proportionate value.

At the end of Elizabeth's reign, chairs began to be made in greater numbers and with some consideration for the comfort and convenience, as well as the dignity, of the sitter. A standard type without arms appeared for the first time, with seat and low back upholstered in a fabric with a knotted pile, called 'Turkey' work, which, in spite of its name, was of native manufacture and fairly expensive. These chairs were strongly constructed of oak or beech, with turned legs and stretchers. Known as 'farthingale' chairs, they are said to have been first introduced to meet the requirements of the ladies, whose fashionably enormous skirts, supported on an unyielding framework, made it impossible for them to sit in a chair with arms.

To me, it seems quite extraordinary that it should have needed an exaggerated fashion in women's clothes to bring about the manufacture of a chair without arms. In fact, the design of clothes has often affected that of furniture to a remarkable extent.

Farthingale chairs were not, at first, made in sets. I have seen a few pairs, but mostly they were constructed singly until some time towards the middle of the seventeenth century, when the habit grew—regrettably, I sometimes think—of making whole families of chairs, all looking like identical twins. Personally, I find it rather dull to have six or eight or even a dozen chairs, all exactly alike. It is also difficult, not to say expensive, to find a really fine set, of any period prior to Victorian, all in a reasonably good state of repair, and the more chairs there are in a set, the more they are worth per chair.

I am constantly trying to talk people into buying *odd* chairs —odd in the sense of single, not queer, specimens—of whatever style and period appeals to them, so that the final result is a subtly varied collection of antiques in itself. In this way, very much better chairs can usually be acquired for much less money; if a method of unifying them is felt to be necessary, then upholster them, if you must, all to match. Fortunately, perhaps, very few people take my advice about collecting a harlequin set, so there are still a great many fine old chairs to be bought at a fraction of the price they would command if comprising part of a set.

Another advantage of variety in dining-chairs is the private joke to be enjoyed when planning places at table: provide each guest with a chair to suit him, or her—the one with the well-shaped legs for that very attractive woman your wife isn't too happy about, the specimen that squeaks in protest for Cousin Maude, and the stiff-backed example with too much upholstery for your mother-in-law. The possibilities are endless. You could even have a Savonarola model—both folding and fixed types were current in late sixteenth- and early seventeenth-century England—for Madam X.

One of the more important features in the home at that time was a 'cupboard' for the display of wealth in the form of silver —literally, a board for cups, in the form of a side-table with turned legs and square stretchers below. One layer of family plate proving inadequate in prestige-value among the more prosperous, extra shelves were added. Three shelves in all are usual, but specimens with up to six tiers are recorded. Part of the space between the shelves was sometimes enclosed with panels and a door, and so a 'cupboard' came to mean a space enclosed by a door.

The open, three-tiered 'cupboard', completely unenclosed, is often described, inaccurately, as a 'buffet', and the type entirely closed as a 'court cupboard'. These misnomers have come to be so generally accepted that there is little point in trying to correct them here. Pedants are referred to *Antiques Today*,[1] in which I made an attempt to sort out the different terms for the various kinds of 'cupboard', and the ways in which they have changed their meanings.

The three-tiered 'buffet', so-called, or open court cupboard, can take its place in many a modern home—if not for the accommodation of the tribal trophies then for one or two *objets d'art*, and perhaps a few books, the electric toaster and a bag of mints. One fault common to many designers of modern furniture is that they insist on a place for everything, but fail to provide us with roomy, casual dumping-grounds for our odds and ends. You just can't dump happily or even efficiently on a room-divider. If you do, what is dumped from Division A is in grave danger of falling to the floor in Division B. On the sort of thing I've been describing, and which you can see in Plate VIA, you can dump away to your heart's content.

The enclosed type of standing-cupboard—popularly called a 'court cupboard'—is even more useful, providing wonderful storage and wasting no space. It has the added advantage of

[1] J. Garnet Miller, 1960.

being too heavy for women to move it about every five minutes. Two men can cope fairly easily, when it is empty. The thing to do is to get the chap next-door to come in when you're both gardening, to give you a hand. Make sure there is a reasonable amount of mud on both your boots (yours and his, I mean), that comes off, in the course of the operation, over the carpet. When the thing has been moved to the place where the little woman wants it to be, both men must appear quite exhausted. The neighbour must be asked to sit down and light his pipe—a really foul one, if it can be managed—while bottles of beer are brought out. Make a session of it. You'll get black looks from milady for days, but you won't have to move the court cupboard again for months.

This type of cupboard has doors above and below, with a cornice that sometimes projects and is supported at each end by a turned column. In later versions, this turning shrinks to a pendant, pointed knob. (See Plate VIB.)

The enclosed cupboard was made from Elizabethan times onwards, throughout the seventeenth century, and in the more remote districts—especially in Wales—it continued as a household favourite until the middle of the eighteenth century. It seems gradually to have been ousted from popularity by the dresser (see pp. 159, 160).

Jacobean. In the early seventeenth century, the side-table frequently had three drawers fitted to it, side by side, and was then known by the name of 'dresser' because, like the open court cupboard, it was 'dressed' with the domestic silver. Originally, it had no shelves above. This feature was a later development, dealt with on p. 160. The drawer-fronts of the Jacobean dresser were decorated with rather heavy mouldings, arranged geometrically, in the manner of the Northern Netherlands (see p. 55).

Another favourite form of Jacobean decoration was split turnery. Pieces of wood were turned on the lathe and then sawn vertically down the centre, the flat surfaces then being glued to the panels of doors or chests, or even to the framework itself.

Chests now came in for a good deal of attention. They continued to be made, as always, on the box principle, but like the French 'coffre', acquired drawers and became, first, a mule-chest, and second, a chest-of-drawers (see Fig. 9). Various explanations are given for the name 'mule-chest'. My own, recently invented and supported by absolutely no evidence whatsoever, is that the joiners' early, crude attempts at making drawers resulted very often in a bad fit. The drawers stuck, refusing to move however hard one tugged or pushed—as obstinate as mules!

Perhaps I should add that the usual explanations of the origin of the term include the obvious one that the mule-chest is, like a mule, a mongrel, being half box-chest and half chest-of-drawers; secondly, that chests were also used as travelling trunks and were often carted on mule-back; thirdly, that the word mule is, in this context, a corruption of 'newel', and that the 'mule-chest' originally stood near the newel-post. This last one was, if I remember rightly, another of my own romances, but I have now abandoned it in favour of the obstinate-as-a-mule theory. If it has any substance, there are a lot of modern pieces with fast-sticking drawers that ought to be called mule-chests.

The early seventeenth-century chest-of-drawers proper, with its moulded drawer-fronts, seldom gives trouble of this kind. The joiners soon learned to make them smooth-running, grooving the sides of the drawers so that they ran on guides. This method continued until a little after 1700, when it was discarded in favour of runners and guides below the drawers.

These early chests-of-drawers in oak are less popular, today, than the later ones of walnut and mahogany—yet there is much to be said for them, as they are usually only three feet across, and low enough to be used as dressing-tables.

Carolean. During the early years of Charles I, England was making steady progress in the domestic arts, and the more splendid houses, at least, were probably much more comfortable than one might suppose from looking at most of the furniture which has survived. Richly upholstered settees with high backs and hinged arms, such as those at Knole, from which they take their name, may well have been fairly plentiful—at least in the homes of those rich enough to afford the high prices of imported velvets. The value lay entirely in the upholstery, which inevitably wore out, rather than in the beechwood frames, prone to attack by wood-worm and doubtless not considered worth recovering. Few genuine examples of fully upholstered chairs and couches of the period have, therefore, survived, and the buyer should be wary of any items of this kind offered to him as 'genuine Carolean'.

It is virtually impossible, even for the expert, to judge whether a *fully upholstered* frame is an authentic antique, without first removing some, at least, of the covering.

Quite apart from the decay that inevitably destroys, over the years, some of the more delicate fabrics, a great deal of wanton destruction occurred during the Civil War that brought the reign of Charles I to its tragic end. Whatever faults this king displayed, at least insensitivity to the arts was not among them. He was, in fact, the first English king seriously to collect paintings and take a real interest in the furnishing of the royal palaces. It is our abiding loss that his collection was dispersed by the Council of State, and so many of the very fine things that must have existed became scattered and lost.

Perhaps the most interesting, to us, of the articles of furniture surviving from Carolean times are a number of oak arm-chairs having no upholstery, the seats being of wood. Fitted with a velvet-covered cushion—of foam-rubber, if you like—they are not uncomfortable, and certainly they are handsome. The backs are fairly low and are usually finished with a cresting rail decorated with carving. This largely ornamental feature is usually plonked on top of the uprights of the back, and not set between them as had previously been the case. This method of setting the cresting-rail on to, rather than between, the uprights is technically important, because it is one that dominated English chair making for a long time—until the end of the eighteenth century, in fact. In Carolean examples, it often projects sideways beyond the uprights, a shaped and carved bracket being set in the outside right-angle so formed (Fig. 11). The back is filled in with a wooden panel, either plain or carved, the arms are open and curve steeply down to be supported by bulbous turnings matching the legs. Dated examples are sometimes found, but Victorian fakes are also plentiful. These latter are usually to be recognized by an excess of bad carving, the use of black stain and a certain grotesque quality that never seems to be present in the real thing.

Cromwellian. A chair of similar proportions, but with seat and back covered in leather, and with bobbin turnings in place of the bulbous variety, appeared after the Civil War. Chairs of a similar type, but without arms, were made to match. Perhaps it was the Puritan psychology that caused chairs of a monotonous sameness to be made in sets. The leather is often stretched across seat and back, without any stuffing under it, and is held in place by large-headed nails or, as they are commonly called, 'studs'.

Chairs of this type were often used in conjunction with the gateleg table—apparently an English invention of about 1650. This does not mean, of course, that every old gateleg table you see is as old as that. Indeed, they are still made in much the same way as they were then, so it is hardly necessary, here, to describe their construction in detail. Distinguishing a genuine example from an oldish reproduction is not always easy, and it is of some importance to be able to do so in this case, as gateleg tables are popular items for use in modern rooms where space is at a premium. Points to look for are the fixing of the oval or circular top to the frame with dowel-pins, and signs of wear on the feet of the gates, where they have been dragged across the floor on countless occasions for the erection of the flaps. There should also be evidence of wear on the upper surface of the stretchers which join the legs to each other near the floor, as a natural consequence of having been used as foot-rests. The same argument applies here as with the stretchers of joyned stools (see p. 60), and the same care should be exercised to detect genuine wear from the faker's ploy with spokeshave and rasp.

In the 1930's, I visited a London furniture factory specializing in reproduction furniture. To get through the main entrance, I had to climb on to, walk across and descend from a gateleg table that had been placed uncompromisingly in the doorway. The proprietor explained that this table had been returned for the fourth time by a customer because it did not look old enough. It had been subjected to all the normal ageing processes—known technically as 'distressing'—including being fired at with a shot-gun. At his wits' end, the poor man had now put the table in its present position, so that everyone going in and out of the factory, including the staff of about fifty people, were obliged to trample over it. If this proves anything, it is that faking antiquity is not easy, but that there are people prepared to go to some pains to achieve it, and anyone relying on the inexpert appraisal of surface appearances is really courting trouble.

In spite of all this, perfectly genuine examples of the gateleg table are still to be bought at quite sensible prices. Some repair will almost always be necessary, if it has not already been carried out, as this is the kind of article that has had to endure heavy wear, even if fifty people haven't been walking over it night and morning. Though the first gatelegs were made in Commonwealth times, the greater number that survive date from the late seventeenth or eighteenth centuries. The turning of the legs is the best indication of date. Those with 'barley-sugar' twists are always after 1660.

Restoration. It was in that year that Charles II returned from exile on the Continent to occupy the throne of England. Reaction from Commonwealth austerity, aided and abetted by continental ideas of domestic luxury, is very marked in much of the furniture made during the next few years, but it would be very wrong to assume that every craftsman and all his customers allowed themselves to be unduly influenced by the change. Indeed, one must always be on one's guard against dating pieces strictly according to whatever fashion prevailed in London. In the provincial towns, and to an even greater extent in rural areas, there was always a conservative tendency to go on making things in the traditional way for a long time, tardily introducing features which had, in the metropolis, already ceased to be 'in the mode'. (I am told that the same sort of process, greatly accelerated, occurs today in the field of women's clothes.) Country-made furniture usually exhibits a certain simplicity—an almost naïve quality that makes it readily distinguishable from the more sophisticated London product. In dating it, look for the latest feature, estimate the approximate date it was fashionable in the capital, and add on twenty-five years for luck. (See Chapter Seven.)

While simple English styles continued to serve for much of the honest furniture made for honest folk, during the forty-two years between the accessions of Charles II and Anne a complexity of foreign influences nevertheless made itself evident, especially on that produced for the great houses. Many of the techniques and ideas of design, construction and finish which were current in continental work were now learned by English craftsmen, who enjoyed a boom in trade following the Great Fire of London. Thousands of homes were destroyed, and in replacing their furniture, the majority of citizens either asked for, or were persuaded into taking, things in the new fashion rather than the old. For this reason, there was very much more new furniture made in London between 1665 and 1670 than there would otherwise have been.

Walnut now became the most popular wood, used in the solid for the frames of tables, chairs, stools, day-beds and cabinets, and in the form of veneer for flat surfaces such as doors, drawer-fronts, and the tops of tables and chests-of-drawers.

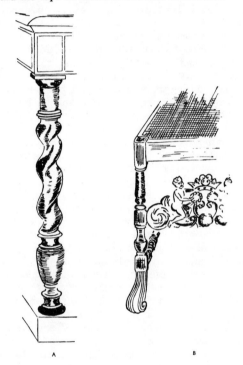

A   B

FIG. 12

Legs of the Restoration Period
A. The 'barley-sugar' twist, introduced into Britain about 1663.
B. Turned chair-leg ending in 'Braganza' foot, with attached front stretcher carved in the 'boyes and crowne' fashion which marked the restoration of the monarchy in 1660, but continued in use for some years after.

Cane was woven in small mesh for the seats and backs of chairs. Chair-backs changed abruptly from the low, square shape of the Commonwealth to tall, narrow frames with central panels of cane-work and surmounted by cresting-rails which were almost invariably arched and were often elaborately carved. The stretcher between the front legs was similarly shaped, and placed rather higher than the turned stretchers of preceding years. (One reason for this was that the floors were now being swept more frequently, and the front rail no longer served the function of a place to hitch your feet.) The motif of a crown supported by a couple of cherubs is a favourite theme for the carver of these cresting-rails and front stretchers. This type of chair was made in sets, both with and without arms; when present, the arms are of bold scroll-shape and left open. Scroll-shapes also appear in the framing of the central panel of the back, and occasionally in the Braganza foot (Fig. 12B), but legs themselves remained vertical until after 1680; although there was no curve in the *line* of the leg until after that date, there was no lack of profile, legs being turned in a great variety of patterns—baluster, columnar, bobbin, and 'barley sugar' twist (Fig. 12A).

The twist is essentially a Baroque motif, being derived from Spanish-Moorish architecture, probably introduced into England when Katherine of Braganza furnished her rooms at Somerset House with furniture from her own country, *circa* 1663. At first, the English craftsmen carved the twist laboriously by hand, but once having learned to turn it on the lathe, they seem to have fallen very much in love with it, their affection proclaiming itself in intricate variations that included the double and even the open twist. This fragile, hollowed-out version was carved out of the solid, and was often used, improbably, for supporting quite heavy carcases in the form of cabinets and chests. The English were a little cautious in their handling of the Baroque, accepting, to a large extent, the discipline imposed on the style by Louis XIV and his designers. Exploitation of the twist was carried to a greater extent, perhaps, than any other Baroque mannerism, in the construction of English furniture for everyday use.

Greater latitude was indulged in when devising decorations for the mansions of the rich and, of course, the palaces of the king. Even so, and despite Charles II's reputation as the Merry Monarch, the Baroque remained, even at its most exuberant, a solemn style, aiming at grandeur rather than gaiety. This is clearly to be seen in the highest attainment of British Baroque —woodcarving in the Italianate manner.

Its chief exponent was the famous Grinling Gibbons (1648–1720) who enjoyed royal patronage under Charles II, James II, William and Mary, Anne and George I. His style was ornate, his mastery of technique superb, so that he could carve great garlands of flowers the petals of which appear about to fall, their stems tied by ribbon so slender, one expects it to snap under the strain. The west chimney-piece of the saloon at Belton might, it must be confessed, have served very well as a shop-front for a very high-class licensed dealer in game. Gibbons carved every feather on every dead bird with the utmost precision. Some of his most attractive work was done at this and other country houses, particularly Petworth. Actually there is very little documentary proof that Gibbons executed much of the work attributed to him, apart from that carried out in the royal palaces, and certainly there were other carvers in his day who worked with him and adopted his style. Very little furniture can be said to have been carved by the master himself. His work is largely confined to architectural woodwork, much of it executed under the direction of Hugh May and Christopher Wren. It was seldom that Gibbons squandered his great talents on anything less than a magnificent frame for a ducal portrait or an altar for the royal chapel.

Such things are, admittedly, of little practical interest to the owner of a small *bijou* residence, but there are, nevertheless, many small and attractive items of Restoration furniture, some of them carved by lesser men in the Gibbons manner, which lend themselves very well indeed to modern use. Chairs of the high-backed, narrow-seated variety described on p. 69 are difficult to find in sets, but odd ones are excellent for the small bedroom or entrance-hall, as they take up very little space. As dining-chairs, they are less satisfactory. Their construction is not always very strong, they tend to tip backwards too easily, and when a number of them are placed around a table, they form, by virtue of their high backs, a rather formidable fence. If you should acquire the odd specimen with damaged cane-work, this can usually be replaced by blind craftsmen, who are highly skilled at the work, though employing a rather wider mesh than was usual in the seventeenth century. Alternatively, this type of chair can be upholstered in velvet, as many were when first made.

Mirror-glass had been made successfully for the first time in England during the reign of James I, at Southwark—Venice having previously enjoyed a near-monopoly. The venture seems to have dwindled away during the Civil War and the Commonwealth—perhaps a puritanical fear of vanity as a sin may have had something to do with it. Now, with the encouragement of the Crown, the industry got going again, and a new factory was established at Vauxhall. The size of the sheets was, however, somewhat limited, and most of the looking-glasses that have survived from that period are attractively small. The frames are sometimes of carved wood—walnut or gilt—and sometimes of simple, flat construction, covered over with needlework. Stuart needlework is distinctive and pleasing, and when used for mirror-frames in this way, it has often survived the passage of time pretty well, not having been subjected to hard wear-and-tear. When padded up to give a three-dimensional effect, it is called 'stump work'.

Bed-covers and hangings of Stuart embroidery, or 'crewel-work', are also sometimes to be found in fairly good state. They were often the best thing in the Charles II bedroom, with the possible exception of Nell Gwyn. In most Stuart homes, the bedroom did not come in for much attention, from the furnishing point of view. Such needlework is always worth acquiring, even if only small sections can be salvaged for covering stools and making lamp-shades. This sounds terribly arty-crafty and straight from the women's magazines, I know, but I can't help it. It's true.

Despite the generally sparse furnishing of the Restoration bedroom, chests-of-drawers—often veneered in walnut and sometimes with elaborate marquetry—were made in ever increasing numbers, while small toilet-tables made their appearance, usually having one drawer and standing on turned legs joined below by stretchers. In the earlier and simpler examples, these stretchers follow the rectangular shape of the top, but by about 1680, they began to take the form of a flat, X-shaped cross, so that each leg is joined to that diagonally opposite. This feature is not only more pleasing to the eye, but gives space for the feet when sitting at the table. It was a method of construction directly imitated from Louis XIV furniture. (Fig. 14E.)

Another craze copied from the Continent was for the ubiquitous cabinet-on-stand. It was the version in oriental lacquer which first became fashionable in England, in the 1660's. The commonest ground colour is black, the richest—red. Other colours are green, creamy-white, and—very rare—blue. Over the ground-colour, a Chinese or Japanese scene is painted in gold. These cabinets had been finding their way into Britain since Elizabethan times, but it was not until the monarchy had been restored that the passion for displaying them in the Louis XIV manner, mounted on carved stands, really got under way. Like their European counterparts, they are fitted with a pair of doors which conceal a multitude of small drawers (see p. 36). The lacquer cabinet was customarily mounted on a stand of distinctly European flavour that hardly ever introduces any oriental motifs, being richly carved with foliage, flowers and cherubim in the best Italian Baroque manner, and either gilded or—more rarely—silvered.

These stands sometimes turn up minus the cabinet but plus a marble top, and as such they make splendid side-tables—provided one has a room of sufficiently generous proportions to take so showy an item. From the serious collector's point of view (and how damned serious some collectors are!) a side-table that started life in this way, as a stand for a cabinet, is supposed to be worth less money than one which was intended from the outset to be a table. Frankly, I can't see why this should be so, since cabinet and stand were separate pieces in the first place. It is really only the marble top which does not belong, and this has very often had to be replaced anyway, even when the table really was a table originally—if you can possibly see what I mean. I heartily dislike the mutilation of old furniture so that it can be made, ruthlessly, to serve modern needs, and I would quite cheerfully strangle the man who thinks nothing of tearing all the little drawers out of one of these cabinets to make room for cocktail equipment or hi-fi mix-ups.

On the other hand, it is foolish to become too pedantic and disparage a perfectly good article that, for one reason or another, is no longer serving the purpose for which it was made, having been parted at some time from the article it was meant to complement. I infinitely prefer the innocent party, divorced from its mate, to the co-called 'married piece' composed of parts of two or more entirely separate pieces, re-assembled with varying dergees of skill. The results of some of these unions really are highly improper. They appear to be not so much married as living in sin.

James II (1685-1689). By the time Charles was succeeded by his brother James, the popularity of lacquer—not only for cabinets but for many other items, too—was so extensive that it was being strenuously imitated in Britain. 'Japanning', as it was called, was executed not only by professionals but by ladies of quality, who took it up as a pleasant change from embroidery and coquetry. This accounts for the enormous difference in quality to be seen in examples of English lacquer work. The English are incorrigible amateurs in the truest sense. The idea that they have no real appreciation of the arts is entirely fallacious. They adore the arts. It is the professional artist of whom they are suspicious, regarding him as an unnecessary expense so long as Alice is there with her water-colours and Henry can take enough time off from the office to write the play for the dramatic society *and* construct the scenery.

At a time when those with a social conscience were really very worried indeed about the religious convictions of their king —James was a Roman Catholic, and had Grinling Gibbons decorate a fine new chapel for him at Whitehall—at this very same time, the more frivolous-minded were recklessly 'japanning' everything in sight, and just as this book is, oddly enough, one of a series that gives the amateur instructions on everything from arranging flowers to building a radio telescope, so, in 1688, John Stalker and George Parker published their *Treatise of Japanning and Varnishing*. This has recently been reprinted in facsimile, with illustrations, and makes fascinating reading.[1]

To make things just a little more complicated, it was not unusual to ship consignments of English-made furniture— especially clock-cases—to the East for lacquering, and bring them all the way back again.

We thus have four main classes of lacquered furniture being produced at much about the same time: first, the completely oriental product; second, the English product lacquered in the orient; third, the English product 'japanned' in England by professionals; and fourth, the English product 'japanned' by amateurs.

[1] Tiranti, 1961.

Sorting them all out is, frankly, not one on which precise directions for doing it yourself can be given, but in the main, it is quality that counts. The entirely Chinese work is really the best, although top-class English specimens are much sought after and have been known to bring very high prices indeed. The actual processes were different, and different materials were used, but it requires experience to recognize the distinctions. An indication that can usually be relied upon is that genuine Chinese lacquer shows a brownish colour where worn, and the portrayal of oriental scenes is naturally much more convincing.

All types which I have mentioned were essentially plain surfaces with decoration painted on in gold so heavily that it is actually raised above the surface. There is yet a fifth class of lacquer-work, in which the decoration is *incised*. This is known as Coromandel lacquer, and so far as I am aware, there were no European substitutes. It mostly arrived in Europe in the form of screens, but these were sometimes broken up and the panels used for cabinets. This practice was much more common, however, in France, at a rather late date.

The Chinese also made for themselves, and to a limited extent for export, a wonderful red lacquer which is minutely carved. It is most often encountered in the form of small, circular boxes, but substantial items of furniture—beds, chairs and tables—were made. Early examples are of superb workmanship and rich in colour. The best period is that of the Ming (1368–1644), but fine work was produced until 1869, when the imperial factories were burned down. The period of K'ang Hsi (1662–1722), which is the one we are concerned with at the moment, was notable for its lacquer, and perfectly genuine specimens are still to be bought, in Europe, for less money than the English imitations of the Stalker and Parker variety often bring.

Torchère stands of various forms, to support candelabra, began to appear about this time, and one colourful type was richly decorated in lacquer and enamel. These are carved in the round to represent negroes or Indians—usually male—and are also found as supports for small tables. Whether any were actually made in England is doubtful. It is much more likely that they were imported from Italy and Germany, and there is some evidence that certain types came from India. These 'blackamoors' or 'Nubian slaves', as they are called, reflect the fashion begun in the second half of the seventeenth century for employing negro servants and page-boys. Many were probably used less as domestic pieces than as display-stands in the shops of tobacconists and others importing exotic commodities. They continued to be made over a very long period, certainly as late as the mid-nineteenth century. These later examples have a distinctly nineteenth-century look about them, and the lips are realistically modelled to negroid form, while the earlier specimens have thin lips. Regency examples are sometimes life-size, but I have seen Charles II blackamoors that, either in pairs or singly, are small enough to decorate the entrance hall of a luxurious flat very effectively indeed. The later and larger types belong, I think, where one usually sees them—in film-sets of night-clubs.

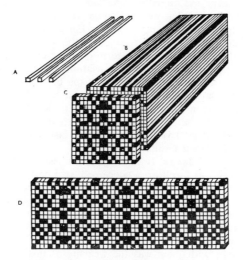

Fig. 13

Tunbridge Mosaic Inlay

Wooden strips of square section, (A), are glued together lengthwise to form a solid block, (B). According to the pattern desired, so the colours of the strips are arranged. The block is now sawn into slices, so that a series of identical cross-sections (C) can be laid side by side to form a continuous pattern, (D).

They somehow manage to hint at vice without being actually pornographic.

Another specialized subject which can be traced back to Charles II's time is Tunbridge ware. This comprises a large class of work, made over a period of about two centuries. Most of the products were small—tea-caddies, lace boxes, etc., and seldom anything larger than a work-table—the principle being that they were made as gifts and souvenirs for the visitors who came to take the waters. Tunbridge Wells had been a health-resort of modest size until the influx of visitors during the Great Plague of 1664. Little cabins mounted on wheels or sledges, something akin to modern caravan-trailers, were brought in to accommodate this population, and permanent guest-houses built. Cashing in on the plight of London, the local tradesmen developed their craft of turnery and miniature woodwork, selling the products to the rich refugees. What we think of as 'Tunbridge ware' did not appear until the following century. Early in the eighteenth century, an Italian workman settled in the town and began to decorate the local work with a form of inlay, closely related to parquetry (see p. 116) and other variations of inlay work. The method was to glue together thin strips of wood, of square section and variegated colour, to form a solid block. Cross-sections were then sawn off to form veneers which could be set edge to edge, to build up a mosaic pattern (Fig. 13). Roughly speaking, the period of Tunbridge ware lasts from the Great Plague to the Great Exhibition.

The reign of James II hardly constitutes a self-contained 'period', so far as furniture is concerned. It is best regarded as a continuation of the Restoration during which the continental influence, already powerful, was given a further boost by the fresh influx of foreign workmen—the Huguenots who were fleeing France and taking refuge in Holland and Britain (see p. 49). Perhaps the most important of the industrial techniques they brought with them was the weaving of textiles, with the direct result that it now became possible for chairs and settees to be upholstered in fine fabrics far less expensively than hitherto. Imported velvets had always been expensive—now they were deliberately made almost prohibitive by a protective tariff, slapped on by the British Government to help the new ventures in weaving at home.

Unfortunately, few seventeenth-century pieces survive with their original covers intact and usable, but modern equivalents are very good, and the re-upholstery of antique chairs, provided it is carried out by an expert, does not, in the ordinary way, reduce their value. I would stress the importance of employing the skilled upholsterer; there is, currently, a great vogue among housewives for attending evening classes and then proceeding to operate on the drawing-room chairs. Much depends on the housewife, the evening class and the chairs in question, but in many cases these good ladies do untold damage, some of it irreparable. The less skilful should do as James II was obliged to do—abdicate!

William and Mary (1689-1702). Continental influence had been strong enough, goodness knows, on much of the furniture of the Restoration. With the coming of the Huguenots, it was given a further impetus, and when James's daughter Mary ascended the throne with her Dutch husband, William of Orange, in 1689, the pressure really became intense. It was not just one influence, but many—a rush of separate currents, all combining to sweep the insular shores of Britain in a flood-tide of exuberance.

If you have read this chapter so far without becoming hopelessly confused—and if you have, you're doing better than I am—you will, at this point, be able to appreciate that the English furniture makers were now having to contend with ideas arriving, directly and indirectly, from Holland, France, Italy, Spain, Portugal, India, and China. To give but one example, the *style Louis Quatorze*, with Italian origins and oriental overtones, had been taken to Holland by men like Daniel Marot, there subjected to modifications to suit Dutch taste—itself already conditioned by the Spanish occupation with its Moorish inheritance—and was now brought to Britain by William and Mary and their Dutch following. What is more, it had to be grafted on to the Anglicized version of itself that had already existed for a quarter of a century. The really astonishing thing is that, as we shall presently see, all this sorted itself out in another fifteen years, and a style unmistakably English emerged.

In the meantime, the rich and abundant William and Mary period itself offers much that is of practical interest to the modest home-maker (see Fig. 14). Bureaux, bureau-bookcases and cabinets for china were now made, in anything like quantity,

Fig. 14

The William and Mary Period

A. Walnut bureau-bookcase with double-dome top and bun feet.
B. Star-and-and-drop handle.
C. Diagram showing, in cross-section, method of fitting this type of handle.
D. Cushion mirror decorated with marquetry.
E. Table with marquetry top, on scroll legs.
F. Detail of characteristic design for the corner of a table decorated with marquetry.
G. Detail from top corner of an escritoire, showing moulding of cornice, convex-fronted drawer in frieze, and herring-bone cross-banding.
H. Turned legs of 'inverted cup' style.
I. Chair-back shewing early version of vase-shaped splat.

for the first time in England. Characteristic features are 'double dome' tops to the bureau-bookcases and the use of mirror-glass in their doors. Wall-mirrors are rectangular with wide frames of convex section, veneered in walnut or lacquered. Known as 'cushion' mirrors, the demand for them seems to be limited, at the time of writing, and good examples can be bought very reasonably. These mirrors were sometimes, if not always, originally fitted with a decorative cresting piece, but it is very often absent today, and the plain, rectangular shape is very pleasing without this embellishment. More fashionable are the toilet-mirrors fitted to a stand with a nest of drawers below, that made their début at this time, and served as a theme for variations ever after. Used in conjunction with the toilet-table of the day, they still serve admirably as dressing-tables, and it is no exaggeration to say that some of the most pleasing and useful furniture for the bedroom was made during the William and Mary period.

Especially good are the chests-of-drawers, 'highboys' and 'lowboys'. Most of the fine ones were made, basically, of pine, with oak-lined drawers, and were veneered in walnut and other finely figured woods, such as yew-tree, burr-elm and laburnum. (An account of veneering as a technique is given on pp. 45 and 46, but it should be added here, with special reference to laburnum, that this wood was used at the end of the seventeenth century to achieve a curious effect. Cross-sections were cut from saplings and small branches, producing circles of veneer anything from one inch to six in diameter. These were built up into a pattern reminiscent of a dish of sea-food—from which peculiarity the technique is known as 'oyster' veneering.) On the finer pieces, both floral and 'sea-weed' marquetry were employed, frequently on an ebony ground with a walnut surround.

The William and Mary chest-of-drawers proper was mounted on bun-shaped feet, the drawers being fitted with brass 'pear-drop' handles (Fig. 14). These are fixed by means of two thin strips of brass, pushed through a hole from the front, bent back flat against the reverse side of the drawer-front, and secured with small pins.

The highboy—or tallboy—and the lowboy were simply chests mounted on stands of varying heights, the legs providing a useful clue to the date. Typical leg-shapes of the period are shown in Fig. 14 and it is a fairly safe bet to assume that, flagrant copies apart, they were not much used on London-made furniture after the end of William III's reign. (Country-made versions in oak, of course, must be regarded in the light of the observations made on p. 157.) The relatively short life of these Dutch leg-shapes particularly applies to the turned leg with the inverted cup protuberance and to the double-scroll leg. Though we think of them as Dutch, both forms were in fact, borrowings from the French *style Louis XIV* (see p. 50). The scroll-leg, though it barely survived the seventeenth century in its original form, was shortly to evolve into the cabriole—a smooth, S-shaped curve—which dominated the first half of the eighteenth century, as we shall see in the next chapter.

America

Furniture made by the early settlers in the second half of the seventeenth century follows closely that of the parent nations. English and Dutch styles predominate, with French influence often marked. It seems fairly certain that the first emigrants from Europe took little furniture with them. The craftsmen among them—and those obliged to become craftsmen if they were to have any furniture at all in their cabins—produced, without actual models, the kind of things they remembered from their homelands. They were too isolated to be much influenced by changing fashions in the countries they had left, so that features memorized from the work of earlier periods—English and Dutch Renaissance styles, in particular—occur in American work of 1650–1700. Nostalgia must often have been a formative influence, the recollection of a chest or chair that had been in his family for a generation or two serving a man as a mental image while he worked.

Oak, pine, and maple were the chief materials that came to hand. Construction was solid and substantial, with simple carving as the usual decoration. This was sometimes brightened with painting in red, yellow and black, the pigments being obtained from local earths.

In most early American homes, there was certainly no profusion of furniture, such essentials as a chest or two to hold clothing and valuables, a few chairs and stools, a table and beds with simple framework having to suffice. The so-called 'Connecticut' mule-chests, decorated with split turnery in the Jacobean manner, and sometimes embellished with solid inlay, seem to me to bear a marked similarity to those made in the Llandovery district, in Wales. Bible-boxes of crudely carved oak, usually dated and bearing the owner's initials, are sometimes spoken of as characteristically American items of the Pilgrim Father period, but they, too, have their exact Welsh counterpart. Early American furniture has something in common with Welsh. There seems to have been the same tough nonconformity in religious feeling and, curiously, the same sense of remoteness from England and independence of fine English ways. Wales never seemed to need an ocean between her and England to keep the latest fashion from London comfortably at bay. (See Chapter Seven pp. 159–163) This similarity in the matter of furniture has been shrewdly recognized and exploited by those who glorify history at the expense of geography, improving their bank balances in the process. More than one American dealer has bought Welsh oak from me, confiding that, once on his side of the Atlantic, it would promptly become 'Early American'.

Perhaps it doesn't matter—so long as the things themselves are honest.

CHAPTER FOUR

Baroque to Rococo

JUST because a new century dawns, it does not necessarily mean that designers rise at the crack of that dawn, bursting with a set of brand new ideas. The eighteenth century is rightly spoken of as the Golden Age of furniture-making, but it must be doubted whether, on 1st January, 1700, the craftsmen of Europe all made good resolutions to devise new forms of unsurpassed elegance.

France

The Régence. At that date, France was still under the political and artistic dictatorship of Louis XIV, and there was little departure from the monumental conception of design until about 1715, when the old devil died. With the possible exception of Madame de Maintenon, everyone was delighted. The king's ambition had brought the country to a state of near-ruin, its extended frontiers a constant temptation to the enemies of France.

Successor to the throne was Louis XV, great-grandson of the old king, but as he was still a minor, his uncle Philip, Duke of Orleans, was accorded the task of ruling the country as regent. Philip's power was, in fact, very limited, and his regency, which lasted for eight years, proved to be a series of well-meant blunders. Our interest in this short epoch of French history is centred on the reaction in taste against the heaviness of the Versailles style under Louis XIV—a reaction which led to a major change in furniture-design throughout Europe.

Its leader was Philip's cabinet-maker, Charles Cressent, who may be said to have created the style we call *Régence*—and if no one minds, we will continue to spell it in the French way, to avoid confusion with the English Regency of a century later.

The most important single aspect of Cressent's work was the switch from rectilinear to curvilinear shapes—not only for legs and other appendages, but also for the actual carcases of many articles. He developed the *bombé commode*, a low chest-of-drawers the front and ends of which swell in serpentine curves longitudinally as well as latitudinally (see Fig. 15). *Bombé*

82

FIG. 15

The Louis XV Period
Early- to mid-eighteenth century French styles, generally following a
sinuous line.
A. *Bombé* commode with ormolu mounts.
B. *Bergère*—cushioned arm-chair.
C. *Secrétaire* with fall-front and *chinoiserie* marquetry decoration.
D. *Bureau-plat*—flat-topped writing-table.

means, simply, 'swollen', and I have heard pieces of this type
described, coarsely but vividly, as 'pregnant'. When found in its
more extreme form, the shape can be just a little bit repulsive,
like some of Ruben's more obese subjects; but when restraint has

been employed to impart no more than a gentle swell, the result is as pleasing as the sweetly rounded tums of Botticelli's women.

Cressent was also responsible for a greatly extended use of ormolu mounts (see p. 86), so that they became an integral part of the piece, and not mere applied cornerpieces whose first function had been to protect an edge or corner of Boulle-work (see p. 45). Brass-and-tortoiseshell inlay was now largely abandoned in favour of fine marquetry work in a rich variety of woods.

Though not the creator of the Rococo, Cressent cleared the ground and laid the foundations for it in a way that effectively bridged the gap between the style of Louis XIV and that of Louis XV which was about to come into being, so that the *Régence* was a transitional period of the greatest significance. There were, of course, many other *ébénistes* who followed Cressent's lead, and it is always dangerous to attach too much importance to the work of one man, but his place as prime mover in the change from Classical-Baroque grandeur to Rococo lightness and grace can hardly be challenged. His position as cabinet-maker to the Regent ensured for him the authority necessary for putting his ideas into action, and they accorded well with the mood of the day. Everyone was fed to the teeth with Louis XIV's megalomania, expressed in every possible way from bullying to Boulle-work. The French were more than ready for a bit of light-hearted and light-headed nonsense.

Louis XV (1723-1774). They certainly got it, in full measure. The young Louis became king in 1723 and his uncle, Philip of Orleans, died later in the same year. Charles Cressent was still a relatively young man, and his work and that of his contemporaries now received further impetus from the slightly mad inspirations of the goldsmith and architect, Meissonier. He it was who, more than any other individual, dreamed up the manner of the Rococo or—to give it its French name—*rocaille*, meaning rock-and-shell work; though neither rocks nor shells are necessarily to be found in Rococo furniture.

The Baroque had been, originally, a restless spirit, but under the classicism of Le Brun and his school it had become, like any reformed rake, a model of rather depressing propriety. Now, its illegitimate daughter, the Rococo, pirouetted into circulation, apparently free from parental discipline and exhibiting all the waywardness once displayed by the Baroque in its youth, combined with the quaintness inherited from a Chinese mother. Louis XIV, it may be remembered, had shared the seventeenth century passion for oriental art, which is essentially grave in its concept of beauty. Given the Rococo treatment, *chinoiserie* was made as gay and amusing as everything else in the repertoire. The school of Meissonier and all its imitators, from one end of Europe to another, saw the Chinese as funny little men in comic little hats who paddled absurd little boats across laughable little lakes with ludicrous little houses on their banks and witty little waterfalls emptying themselves upstream.

This was the oriental element that, combined with asymmetrically arranged, ragged, C-shaped scrolls, and a generous allowance of rocks, shells, foliage, flowers, and bows of ribbon, went to make up the ornament of the Rococo. All these motifs, and many more besides, found their way on to the superbly made furniture of the Louis XV period. They were sometimes carved, forming part of the outline of such things as mirror-frames and wall-brackets, which were mostly gilded, but they also found a resting-place in flat and gently curving surfaces, by way of marquetry and lacquer decoration. Painting on the wood itself, or on metal panels inserted in the framework of cabinet doors, became a favourite method of embellishment as the style progressed, idyllic scenes in the '*fête galante*' manner of Watteau and his followers being popular subjects. Elaborately shaped china-cabinets with panels signed 'Martin' are not at all uncommon, but most of them that one sees are nineteenth-century copies, 'Vernis Martin' being a patent lacquer, invented by two brothers named Martin, about 1730.

Such elaboration of shape is, however, a most important feature of French Rococo. The emphasis is always on sinuous lines—indeed, it is often difficult to find a straight one in the entire composition of a piece of *Louis Quinze*. Even flat surfaces are avoided like the plague, unless they are absolutely essential to the function of the article, as in the case of a table-top.

The utmost skill was needed for such work, and the leading cabinet-makers were able to demand high prices. Some of the more successful ones made large fortunes. Their guild was powerful and entry into it was difficult. Not all the Paris *ébénistes* belonged to it, those in certain specified districts of the city being exempted from the law which compelled the rest to belong to the guild or seek employment with a master man who belonged already. Members of the guild usually signed their products by stamping their initials into the woodwork in an inconspicuous place. The makers of ormolu mounts, especially the chisellers, also sometimes signed their work—and not only the great ones such as Jacques Caffieri and his son Philippe. Some never signed their work at all.

Ormolu at its best is a form of bronze—an alloy of copper and zinc, sometimes with the addition of tin. The less zinc used in proportion to copper, the better the bronze. In the hands of artists like the Caffieri's, it was subjected to a long and complicated process of modelling, casting, chiselling, bathing in acid, burnishing and, finally, gilding with gold lacquer—the '*or moulu*', or ground gold, that gives it its name. The epitome of French furniture collecting is reached with the acquisition of a piece signed by both cabinet-maker and bronze-maker.

If you are fortunate enough to own a good piece of French furniture, it is always worth looking over it carefully for a mark of this kind, as the commercial value is often enhanced enormously by its presence. You might even be the lucky owner of a *commode* or *bureau-plat* (not a bureau in the English sense, but a flat-topped writing-table) by the greatest of all the Louis XV cabinet-makers, J. F. Oeben, who was appointed *ébéniste du roi* in 1754. He had learned his trade from André Charles Boulle, cabinet-maker to the previous king, and in his turn taught J. H. Riesener, who was to carry on this tradition by receiving the same honour in the next reign. Oeben died before his last great work, a cylinder-top desk for Louis XV, could be finished, and it was completed by his pupil. This piece is to be seen in the Louvre, and a fellow to it, said by some to have been made for the King of Poland, is in London, in the Wallace Collection. By others, it is thought to be a nineteenth-century copy of the finest quality, and is a salutary warning to intending buyers of antique furniture to find out as much as possible about the subject in advance, and then to have a clear understanding of what is claimed by the seller for the article he is offering. It also raises the interesting question—is there a point at which the bogus becomes authentic?

Personally, I think there is. The difficulty lies in knowing just how to define it in each particular case. A Chelsea or Worcester copy of a Chinese, Meissen or Sèvres porcelain plate is, in a sense, a 'fake', but it is genuine enough, and of greater value than the original, to the collector of old English porcelain. Most, if not all, such copies were made as naïve imitations of what were then *contemporary* originals. That is not the same as reproducing, at a later date, things of a past age. Yet, even when this has clearly been the intention, there are many categories of antiques where such reproductions are accepted readily enough as authentic works of art, in their own right. The Chinese were always much given to reproducing the work of earlier periods, while in Europe, from the Renaissance onwards, interest in classical art has been revived from time to time to such effect that vast numbers of imitations, some of them downright slavish, are now old enough to be 'antiques'. It is only long familiarity with this or that department of collecting that enables one to know where to draw the line—and even then, as the years hurry by, the inevitable tendency is for that line to shift, to move forward from 1830 in Chelsea to 1860 in Kensington (see p. 14). There are purists who try to insist that a 'genuine antique' must be, not only of a certain age but also of the period which it *purports* to be. In practice, this does not work out very well, and strictly applied, it would lead to the casting out as unworthy of a great many fine and beautiful things. I have some Wedgwood library busts about a hundred-and-fifty years old, which 'purport' to be Greek bronze. Do I throw them in the ash-can? Loud cries of 'yes' from members of my family who hate the sight of them!

I have digressed a little from the matter in hand because this principle is rapidly becoming a vital one so far as French furniture is concerned, and I want to make it clear that I am not making a special exception of it. The rules of collecting, such as they are, apply to it just as firmly as—if not more so than—to any other branch of connoisseurship. For that very reason, the exceptions to the rules assume a special importance, particularly for the woman who would like one or two good pieces in her drawing-room, but who, by force of circumstance or virtue, is not in so good a position to command masculine purse strings as was La Pompadour.

Prices of the finest eighteenth-century pieces are now astronomical. The record, to date, is held by a *bureau-plat* sold by

Christie's a year or two ago for 35,000 guineas (approximately $105,000). This attractive little item had been stored in a stable not very far from my home for many years. Nobody told me. Well, it's no good shutting the stable door, etc. But I wish I'd opened it.

Exceptional though this sort of price is, it is not at all unusual for pieces of *Louis Quinze* and *Louis Seize* to bring hundreds of pounds apiece, and quite a few bring thousands. Even a generation ago, before the current fashion reached present dimensions, all but the most important pieces could be purchased in Paris very reasonably—for less money, in some cases, than it cost to make them originally, and almost invariably for less than the same shops were asking for new reproductions. But that was thirty years ago, and the ratio is now very different. Today, reproductions are still being made and are on sale all over Europe. They are nothing like as good as those made before the war, and they are more expensive than ever, but the eighteenth-century originals have now come into their own, and the modern copies are, in the main, much cheaper than the genuine article. (This is true of French furniture but not, necessarily, of modern reproductions of English pieces, which are often more costly than the real thing.)

There is, however, another basis of comparison. Fortunately, the lover of French furniture is not restricted to a choice between fearsomely expensive originals and somewhat less costly, but rather garish, modern copies. Following the defeat of Napoleon and the restoration of the French monarchy in 1815, there was a revival of interest in the eighteenth-century styles which continued throughout the nineteenth century and down to the present day. A hundred years and more ago, some really first-class copies were made. True, they lacked originality, but both material and workmanship were as good as that found in the things that inspired them. In fact, blasphemer that I am, I incline to the view that, technically speaking, the best copies made between 1840 and 1870 were superior to the medium-grade originals. In the main, they were not intended to be fakes; a reproduction becomes a fake only when the intention is to pass it off as the original. The men who made them were proud of their skill and often signed their products with their own names, as their forbears had done.

PLATE I (*above*). English Gothic Oak Chest of plank construction, sixteenth century. (*By permission of Mr. Ralph Cox, Lincoln.*) PLATE II (*right*). Italian Baroque Carved Pine Frame, seventeenth century. (*By permission of Mr. T. G. B. Brodie-Smith.*)

PLATE III (*left*). Spanish *Papilera*, mounted on a stand braced with wrought iron, seventeenth century. (*By permission of Mr. David Tron, London.*) PLATE IV (*right*). Indo-Portuguese Cabinet-of-Drawers on stand, of red-wood, seventeenth century. (*By permission of Mr. T. G. B. Brodie-Smith.*)

PLATE V (*right*). English Oak Chair with solid seat and high, panelled back, seventeenth century. (*In the author's possession.*) PLATE VI(A) (*below left*). Welsh Oak Open Court Cupboard with 'cup-and-cover' supports, late sixteenth century. (*By permission of The National Welsh Folk Museum.*) PLATE VI(B) (*below right*). Welsh Oak *Cwpwrdd Deuddarn* (two-part Standing Cupboard), early eighteenth century. (*By permission of the National Welsh Folk Museum.*)

PLATE VII (*left*). English Walnut and Yew-wood Escritoire with drawers below and fall-front writing leaf above, early eighteenth century. (*By permission of Dr. T. L. Morris.*) PLATE VIII (*below*). English secrétaire-sideboard, veneered with olive-wood, mid-eighteenth century. Inset shows the writing leaf extended. (*In the author's possession.*)

PLATE IX. French Landscape-Marquetry Commode in natural and stained pearwood, *bois de citron* and walnut, within bandings of tulipwood and purpleheart, the windows of the houses inlaid with mother-o'-pearl. The ormolu mounts and handles in the classical style, the legs retaining the cabriole curve. Transitional period, Louis XV to Louis XVI, third quarter of the eighteenth century. (*By permission of Monsieur Nogatch, Paris.*)

PLATE X (*left*). English Elbow-Chair in Mahogany, Chippendale period, mid-eighteenth century. PLATE XI (*below*). Dutch *bombé* commode veneered in walnut with rococo handles, mid-eighteenth century. (*In the author's possession*.)

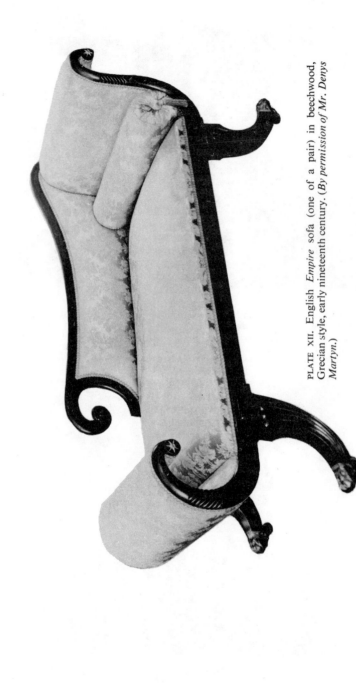

PLATE XII. English *Empire* sofa (one of a pair) in beechwood, Grecian style, early nineteenth century. (*By permission of Mr. Denys Martyn.*)

PLATE XIII (*above*). English Music-Canterbury in rosewood, inlaid with brass, of lyre shape, early nineteenth century. (*In the author's possession.*) PLATE XIV (*below*). Welsh Oak Corner-Dresser, the one side with pot-board and turned columnar legs, the other with enclosed cupboards, on bracket feet, late eighteenth or early nineteenth century. (*Formerly in the author's possession.*)

There is a great deal of this nineteenth-century work about which compares favourably enough with that of a hundred years before, at least from a furnishing point of view, and very favourably indeed with modern reproductions, from *every* point of view, including the financial one, because it is appreciably cheaper than the new and infinitely cheaper than the really old. So far as age is concerned, much of it is now 'antique', according to the more liberal interpretation of the term, and as each year goes by, so more of it passes into this category. Consequently, it is steadily appreciating in value, and good examples command respectable prices.

Of course, however fine a reproduction is, and however mellow the advance of time has made it, it is still a spurious article to the incorrigible seeker after authenticity, who will always prefer a thing to be completely of its own period, however late that period, and however humble the article. There are those who would prefer a simple Victorian kitchen chair of 1860, that doesn't try to be anything else, to a magnificent 1860 copy of a 1760 *fauteuil*. I respect this point of view, and go a long way towards sharing it, but I also sympathize with those prepared to accept the old reproduction that is so good, it needs an expert to tell the difference.

No matter to which of these schools of thought you belong, and even if, like me, you have a foot in each, the great thing, always, is to know what you are about, and to be wary of paying far too much for a reproduction in the mistaken belief that it is a genuine piece going at bargain price. That is the sad but almost inevitable fate of the inveterate bargain-hunter.

Distinguishing between the genuine *Louis Quinze* and the best nineteenth-century copies is not at all easy. The best indications are to be found in the technical methods employed rather than in style. Stylistically, the later pieces are usually fairly accurate, though it is possible to detect, very often, a certain lack of refinement in feeling, a suggestion of vulgarity and flamboyance where there should be an aristocratic elegance. This snobbish approach is not reliable, however, as the same pandering to bourgeois taste is evident in some of the mediocre work of the best periods.

Where methods and materials are concerned, we are on firmer ground, yet even here, quick-sands are there to trap us.

Mid-eighteenth-century furniture was almost entirely hand-made, and the tell-tale marks left by mechanical saws are condemnatory; but their absence is no proof of an early date of manufacture, since many of the nineteenth-century craftsmen disdained the use of machinery. Such marks can also be removed by sandpapering, or covered by veneers. Veneers themselves usually tell us a great deal. In general, old veneers are quite thick—anything up to one eighth of an inch—while those used from about 1840 onwards are relatively thin, modern ones being of paper-thickness. But old veneers may have been rubbed down in the process of re-polishing, giving them a deceptively modern appearance, or transferred from a genuine but unsaleable article to a modern carcase of attractive design. It is easy to be misled, either way, into thinking a piece is older or newer than it really is. Many good judges rightly attach great importance to the quality of the ormolu mounts on Louis XV furniture (see p. 86), which is usually of a high standard on genuine pieces, exhibiting the fine chiselling by hand of the *ciseleur*; whereas the bulk of reproductions lack this finesse, being mounted with bronzes to which little beyond gilding has been done after the casting process. This reliance on ormolu as a guide to genuineness is really rather dangerous, overlooking, as it does, the extremely high standard achieved by some of the copyists. I have also seen relatively modern pieces of good quality with eighteenth-century mounts, doubtless removed from some badly damaged original.

I am sorry if all this sounds thoroughly discouraging, but it would be foolish to pretend that there are any completely safe guides to the recognition of authentic pieces of this or any other period. Experience and the advice of people who have already gained it are the only true guides. Regular visits to the galleries that specialize in French furniture provide the best means of learning. The auction-rooms of London, Paris, and New York can also be very instructive. It should be noted that such shame-making words as 'reproduction' or 'copy' seldom appear in the sale catalogues. Where the piece is described, not simply as 'Louis XV' but 'Louis XV *style*', it is usually safe to conclude that the auctioneers do not consider it to be genuine; the italics, needless to say, are mine.

Style is, however, the first thing to master, and in addition to what I have already said about the general shapes and form of decoration on Louis XV furniture, it might be useful to add a few notes about the individual types that characterize the period (see Fig. 15).

The *commode* has already been mentioned. Usually *bombé* in shape, very often with a marble top, it may be of three-drawer depth, in which case it comes near to the ground; or it may be of two-drawer depth only, and stand on relatively high legs of elegant cabriole form. An important feature of most of the better examples is that the bottom edge of a drawer appears to meet the top edge of the one below it, without any visible dividing rail. The advantage of this arrangement was that the front of the commode could be decorated with lacquer or marquetry, and embellished with ormolu, as though it were one uninterrupted surface. As a girl I know once innocently said, 'I like the French drawers that come down in one piece.'

This leads one, only too naturally, to a recognition of the fact that a great deal of *Louis Quinze* furniture is essentially feminine in character. The king was very much under the influence of his more permanent mistresses, especially Madame de Pompadour —a woman of exquisite taste and high intelligence, whose influence on the arts of the period can hardly be exaggerated in its importance. Many ladies of fashion were not merely literate but literary by aspiration and habit, much given to letter-writing, in the same sort of way as their modern counterparts are telephone-addicts. Pieces of furniture were specially designed to meet their needs, among them being the *secrétaire* and the *bonheur-du-jour*. The former was the first to appear, at the beginning of the reign. It has a fall-front like an English bureau, but it is vertical, not sloping, when in the closed position, with a cupboard enclosed by a pair of doors below. (Somewhat similar pieces, less elaborately shaped, appeared in England during the reign of Anne.) The *bonheur-du-jour* came later, towards the middle of the century, and was so named because it really was the 'success of the day', making an instant appeal as a combined desk and toilet-table. It assumes various shapes, and great ingenuity was often lavished on fitting it out with secret drawers that leap out at the touch of a concealed spring. Essentially, it was a small writing-table with an upper stage comprising a nest of drawers or a cupboard, sometimes enclosed by 'tambour' doors. These are made by mounting narrow slats of wood on to a canvas backing, so that they will run within guides on a curve. Modern roll-top desks, not to mention sliding garage doors, work in much the same way.

The *bonheur-du-jour* probably developed from the *bureau-plat* —the flat-topped writing table—used in conjunction with the *cartonnier*, a nest of open shelves and drawers, rather like the upper part of our old friend the cabinet-on-stand, but without enclosing doors. The *cartonnier* was often most elegantly shaped, with domed top and scrolled ends. Normally it hung from the wall or rested on a side-table near the *bureau-plat*, but there are rare instances of the one being attached to the other, the whole thing conceived as one piece, as was the *bonheur-du-jour*. In its turn, the *bureau-plat* is derived from the Boulle writing-table of the Louis XIV period, and if we go back even farther, we find heavy-looking oak and solid walnut examples of the Louis XIII style (see p. 42) with a nest of drawers fitted to the top. Thus we have the interesting pròcess, over a century or more, whereby the desk with a superstructure of drawers, in a very masculine form, first sheds them and then, ultimately, recovers them in a very feminine form. And while we are being academic, it might be worth mentioning that 'bureau' was originally the name of the cotton material used for covering the tops of desks.

Another instance of a change of meaning is the word '*bergère*'. In its native language, even, it has a fascinating range—shepherdess, nymph, morning cap, wagtail, and cushioned arm-chair. If someone asks a Frenchman if he wants to buy a *bergère*, what does he think is being offered to him? Presumably he just says 'yes', and hopes he won't get a wagtail or a morning cap. Asked the same question, an Englishman could be excused for thinking that the item on the market was an arm-chair—cushioned, certainly, but with caned back and arms, for that is what 'bergère' has meant to the furniture trade in Britain, since the late eighteenth century. Although cane was extensively used in France during the *Louis Quinze* period, the term 'bergère' does not imply the use of it. A *bergère*, in the terminology of French furniture, is an arm-chair with padded back and arms, and a cushioned seat.

In this way, it is distinct from the *fauteuil*—an elbow-chair, with open arms, padded back and seat, and no cushion. Sometimes made with a very deep seat and well-sloped back, as a reclining chair, it is a *fauteuil Voltaire*. The old boy seems to have been something of an authority on the subject, noting that 'ladies can be seen reclining on sofas and day-beds without causing embarrassment to their friends.'

The *Louis Quinze* period produced a great variety of such things. There was the *duchesse*—a day-bed formed by adding one or two extensions to a *bergère*; the *marquise*, a medium-sized sofa with open arms and padded back, and the *panier*, a type with padded back and arms flowing into a continuous curve, so that it forms, as its name suggests, a basket-shape into which the occupant can snuggle very comfortably.

Comfort combined with elegance is the keynote of Louis XV arm-chairs and sofas. One of his daughters remarked that it was only her cosy *bergère* which stopped her from entering a convent. Indulgence in a few such luxuries might well reconcile many a woman to the disappointments and disillusionment of modern life.

There are many more things to choose from, besides the types described above, but some of them are more typical of the next period—the Neo-Classic style of Louis XVI (see p. 115 *et seq.*).

Most styles are continuous, flowing into and overlapping each other, and these are no exception. There was a reaction against the Rococo before the end of Louis XV's reign, and a transitional style had in fact developed as early as what might be called the Pompadour period. It became well established during the years when Madame du Barry was the king's favourite. The process is marked by a gradual return to straight lines and formal decoration. Characteristically transitional pieces retain the flowing line of the cabriole leg, but employ classical motifs for the ormolu mounts. (See Plate IX.)

Such subtleties mostly find expression in the city-made furniture. On p. 48, attention was drawn to the pleasing character of so many of the country-made pieces, and this applies particularly to the *Louis Quinze* style, which continued, so far as they are concerned, with little change, until well into the nineteenth century. I think this continuing popularity may be explained by the fact that the modified Rococo designs of the country craftsmen were essentially more suited to their technical skills than were the Neo-Classic styles, and they had the good sense to go on doing what they could do well, long after their colleagues in the capital had abandoned the Rococo.

As for the rest of Europe, the influence of France was, at mid-century, paramount over the greater part of the Continent. French was the language of diplomacy, and all educated people learned to speak and write it. Many Englishmen, even, were tolerably good at it. Everything in the way of architecture, sculpture, painting, and furniture that appeared at Versailles and in Paris was assiduously copied, or at least emulated, in Berlin, Vienna and St Petersburg. Then—as now—the women of Europe eagerly awaited news of the latest Paris fashions.

National traditions affected design to a greater or lesser extent, peasant pieces retaining their local flavour in all countries, and city-made articles responding very readily to Gallic influence.

Italy

Meissonier himself, 'creator' of the Rococo, was Italian, and Italian versions of '*Louis Quinze*' may be recognized by the extreme forms which the *bombé* curve was wont to take, the extent of the protrusion often being grotesquely out of proportion to the size of the piece. Small commodes with only two drawers, and consequently rather high in the leg, can fit well into the recesses of modern flats, the depth of the recess distracting from the obesity of the piece. These sometimes turn up in pairs and are best used symmetrically, with tall and fairly plain pier-glasses above them to give them much-needed height and dignity.

Some very gay furniture was made in Venice at this period, the entire surface being painted with a ground-colour of pale yellow, apple green or bright blue, with Chinese or floral motifs scattered over it. As the line was sinuous and the surface undulating, the effect is sometimes rather hectic, and the odd-looking settees, chairs, chests-of-drawers, beds, and desks that resulted need placing with great care if the result is not to look like a Venetian carnival. (Of course, you may *want* it to look like that; in which case, the best of Venetian luck to you.) Such pieces have, in the past, been bought very reasonably in English country house sales, and even in London auction-rooms, but the prices have advanced since Italian dealers have been buying up, systematically, the things that left their country many years ago.

Spain

There is some very interesting Spanish Rococo furniture—in

particular, a class that includes commodes, bow-fronted corner cupboards and side-tables, decorated with bone marquetry inlaid into veneers of olive-wood. These pieces are usually described as German, but at least some of them were made in Majorca, and are still to be seen in the palaces of the aristocracy in Palma and in the country houses, the names of which are prefixed by the word 'son', which were used as hunting lodges. The marquetry often illustrates hunting scenes. The *bombé* line is exploited discreetly, in contrast to the usual Italian exuberance described above. Palma has been a great sea-port for centuries, which probably accounts for the amount of this furniture that has found its way to other parts of the world. It has a flavour of its own that may not be to everyone's taste, as the hunting scenes often have a savage quality. Strongly recommended as a presentation piece to a retiring M.F.H.

The *bombé* swell is more pronounced in Rococo furniture of the Spanish mainland, but otherwise the style is often rendered with restraint, and an affinity with English forms of the Queen Anne and early Georgian period is particularly noticeable in the fashioning of chair-drames.

Spanish countrified furniture tends to be more conscious of the Rococo influence than was usual elsewhere outside France, and again it is the chair which demonstrates this most clearly. I have seen some very pleasing examples, attractively small in size and highly suitable for use in the smaller kind of home, with solid seats, cabriole legs joined by under-framing, and backs composed of interlaced curves. They are usually of solid walnut, strongly constructed and very heavy for their size.

Germany and Sweden

The Teutonic and Scandinavian peoples seem to have retained a strong element of the Baroque in their handling of the Rococo, going so far as to apply the twist principle to the new line, so that frame settees appear with double cabriole legs that coil around each other most alarmingly. The hooped frames of chair-backs also double up, with complex carving and fretting between inner and outer frame. An otherwise English-looking chair-back splat was often interpreted with so literal an adherence to the asymmetry of the Rococo that it presents two different profiles. This is not to say that extremely good work was not done in Germany:

on the contrary, some of the leading Paris *ébénistes* were of German origin. More will be said of them in the next chapter, and of their achievement in the reign of Louis XVI.

The Netherlands

Retracing our steps to the end of the seventeenth century, when William of Orange was also King of England, we find, not unnaturally, that many of the forms which furniture took were common not only to these two countries, but also to the American Colonies; but national characteristics very soon asserted themselves, and from the early eighteenth century onwards, the distinctions become fairly clear. The Dutch preference for bold floral marquetry persisted for another hundred years, the importance of flowers to the life and economy of Holland being, perhaps, a conditioning factor. In England, marquetry, as a rule was employed with restraint. In America, it was used hardly at all at this time, although inlaying into the solid, instead of into a veneered ground as in the case of marquetry, was not unusual. The Dutch influence is very marked in much early eighteenth-century American furniture having this kind of decoration, the tulip—for which many an early settler from Holland must have retained a nostalgic affection—being a common device.

Another feature which helps to differentiate Dutch work from English is thicker turning than was customary in Britain. The British have had, from the sixteenth century onwards, a great fondness for wood-turning, and in the early 1700's, they seem to have delighted in reducing the narrow sections to the very minimum, with results not always wholly consistent with practicability. The stretchers which comprise the underframing of Queen Anne chairs have sometimes been fined down to such a degree of slimness on the lathe that they have been unable to withstand the many years of hard wear without snapping. The Dutch employed either thicker turnings, or a flattish, shaped stretcher that was never allowed within reach of a lathe.

As the century progressed, and the sinuous lines of the Rococo wove their way from France across Europe, the Dutch craftsmen adopted the *bombé* shape with enthusiasm but a certain lack of delicacy. Often they used its swelling line for the front only of chests-of-drawers, bureaux and bureau-bookcases, leaving the ends flat. A link between front and end is provided with a broadly canted corner, to which heavily carved paw-feet, in place of French ormolu ones, are affixed. The Dutch version of the *bombé* is often quite distinct from the French in that the swell is lower down the carcase-line, so that the upper half is almost vertical. In the description of the *bombé* form on p. 83, I mentioned that I have heard it termed 'pregnant'; to pursue this figure of speech a little further, the Dutch version is rather that of a pregnancy being carried rather low.

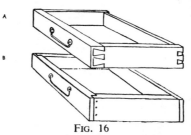

FIG. 16

Methods of Drawer-construction
A. Dovetail joint: the usual English method.
B. Shouldering: more common on continental furniture.

For a few years either way of 1700, there was an Anglo-Dutch class of furniture, some of which defies final analysis. It could have been made in Holland and brought to Britain; it could have been made in Britain by Dutch immigrant craftsmen; or it could have been made by Englishmen closely imitating Dutch models and methods. A useful, but not infallible, indication is the method of jointing the fronts of drawers to the sides. Dutch and German craftsmen often employed what is termed 'shouldering', while the English favoured dove-tailing. (The difference is better explained visually—see Fig. 16.) However, there was a great deal of coming and going and exchanging of ideas, and such points as these must be taken together with the rest of the evidence when inquests are being held. They are the sort of considerations that the modern home-maker, only interested in how the end-product is going to look in the living area of his open-plan maisonette, regards as a crashing bore. But once he gets started on the subject, he will finish up, like the rest of us, contemplating his early eighteenth-century chair with the very

Dutch-looking marquetry in the splat, and the equally English-looking turning of the stretchers, and caring quite passionately whether it started life in Haarlem or Highgate; and he won't be much the wiser for reading this, I'm afraid.

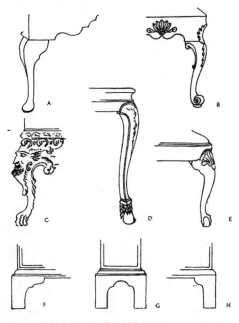

FIG. 17

Queen Anne and Early Georgian Periods
Legs and Feet on early-eighteenth century English Furniture

A. Simple cabriole leg with pad foot.
B. Cabriole leg showing French influence, with scrolled or 'whorled' foot.
C. Elaborately carved leg showing Italian and German influence, with satyr mask on the knee, and paw foot.
D. Elegant form of cabriole leg with pony foot.
E. Characteristic early Georgian form, with shell carved on knee and claw-and-ball foot.
   G and H are variations of the bracket foot, in use throughout the eighteenth century.

Britain

If the chair in question, be it English, Dutch, or anything else, has cabriole legs united by stretchers, it almost certainly belongs to the first twenty years or so of the eighteenth century—unless, of course, it is a downright modern copy. Because its shape necessitates cutting across the grain to some extent, the cabriole leg was at first distrusted by many practical woodworkers. It was, after all, a logical development of the scroll-leg, which had always been provided with underframing, and it was perfectly natural to employ similar precautions with the new, elegant line that first appeared in a pure form about 1700. The more conservative craftsmen continued to use underframing with the cabriole for another twenty years, but adventurous spirits began to discard such clumsy devices early in Anne's reign, allowing the cabriole-legged chair to stand on its own feet, unaided.

Anne (1702-1714). The feet themselves take varying forms (Fig. 17). The commonest is a simple pad. To my taste, it is also the pleasantest. More rarely, we find an English piece of this period with a scroll-foot—either a downward, backward-curving scroll or an upward, forward, curving variety, which sometimes has a peg-like stilt below it, raising it an inch or two above floor-level. Other favourites were carved to represent the feet of animals, a lion's paw or a pony's hoof. This was more or less consistent with the shape of the cabriole leg itself, which really owed its derivation to the use, in classical antiquity, of the goat's leg as a decorative motif. (The recurrence of this form, in its Pan- and other satyr-associations, is an interesting one from which anthropologists with a Freudian turn of mind might well deduce a colourful explanation.) The ball-and-claw foot was also a revival of a very early type. Known to the Ancient Egyptians and Chinese, it first made its appearance on English furniture in the early years of the eighteenth century, and has remained a firm favourite with the manufacturers of dining-room suites down to the present day. It is now so familiar that its rather grotesque and frightening implications do not register with most people, but, Freud apart, I can never look at a well-carved claw-and-ball foot without wincing. I see myself as the ball, and the Tax Collector as the claw. This is not quite the significance intended by the old mythologies, in which the ball symbolized the orb of power, temporal and spiritual, held in the grip of authority. I have often noticed that people with a particular liking for this type of foot also have a liking for power.

The wood-carver exercised great skill on the carving of feet. Often it was his only chance to show his paces, as carving was well-disciplined during the Queen Anne period, seldom being allowed to dominate a piece but used only to provide points of focal interest, such as a shell as the knee-cap of a cabriole leg, or a neat, unobtrusive scroll where the vase-shaped centre-splat of a chair back unites with the swan-necked frame. The emphasis as this time was on elegance of line, strength of construction, good proportions and the fine finish provided by carefully veneered surfaces. Graciousness was supplanting grandiloquence, and masculine solemnity of the Baroque was slowly softening in preparation for the feminine frivolity of the Rococo.

This process began, if anything, earlier in Britain than in France. The English had not been under the dictatorship of Louis XIV, and in moving away from the more ponderous style of the late seventeenth century, the extravagant gestures of the rebel were not necessary to them. The process was gradual— evolution rather than revolution. As a consequence—and perhaps because of a slight check administered with the coming of the House of Hanover in 1714 and the adoption of certain heavier, Germanic forms—English furniture never really tried to be as amusing as did the French work we have considered in this chapter.

Although it is not, at the moment of writing, the most fashionable period, fine-quality pieces of Queen Anne walnut yet command fairly high prices—sometimes very high indeed. This applies especially to the smaller and rarer pieces, such as little bureaux raised on cabriole legs, and 'bachelor' chests-of-drawers with tops of double thickness hinged on the front edge so that they can be extended to rest on sliding supports (technically known as lopers). (See Fig. 18.)

Of the larger pieces, some are considered 'important', e.g. bureau-bookcases in red lacquer. One or two outstanding specimens have been known to bring as much as 5,000 guineas ($15,000) apiece during recent years. Some of the bigger types, however, can be bought at reasonable prices, and the idea that they are out of place in the modern home is fallacious. The double chest-of-drawers, or 'chest-on-chest', which first appeared

FIG. 18

English Furniture, first half of the eighteenth century
A. Chest-on-chest.
B. Mirror in decorated frame with swan-neck pediment.
C. Bachelor chest-of-drawers with top extending forward.
D. Wing arm-chair.
E. Standard-chair, the back with solid centre-splat, shaped seat and cabriole legs.
F. Oval flap-table on cabriole legs.
G. Brass loop-handle and contemporary lock-plate.

in Britain about 1710, is a good case in point. Many dealers find them difficult to sell—even the fine, early examples with beautifully figured walnut veneers—but, in fact, they are great space-savers, occupying no more floor space than would a substantial chest-of-drawers, and providing double the accommodation. Later examples of mahogany, and oak ones of all periods, are in even less demand, although there is considerable interest, in America, in the highboy or chest-on-stand, which actually wastes space, the lower stage consisting mainly of legs which, as often as not, are barely strong enough to support the heavy carcase above. What the poor old chest-on-chest has done to deserve such comparative neglect, I really don't know.

I would, however, offer a word of warning about Queen Anne walnut and, indeed, all veneered furniture. It is broadly true that the finest furniture is veneered, but it can suffer badly from the effects of excessive central heating. In humid heat, veneers lift, because they were originally fixed with animal glue, not the synthetic kind that science has been obliged to perfect in order to combat the destructive properties of the steam-pipes. Often there is unequal expansion and contraction of veneer and solid foundation. Even pieces constructed entirely of solid timber, without any delicate surface of veneer, deeply resent being placed too near a piping hot radiator, and register their protest by splitting—sometimes very noisily, with a crack like a pistol-shot.

Providing you can arrange your life so that the heating arrangements do not engender a tropical temperature, the following types of early eighteenth-century furniture are strongly to be recommended.

During this period, the fashion of dining in small groups, begun in Restoration times, persisted. Although oak gateleg tables continued to be made, they were largely replaced by 'flap' tables, oval or circular when erected, and constructed in solid walnut. These tables have four cabriole legs, two of which are hinged to support the flaps. They fold down to a conveniently small size, and when extended are more comfortable to sit at than the gateleg, having no underframing to get in the way (Fig. 18).

Queen Anne dining chairs, handsome though they are, are less easy to use in a small room, the generous width of the seats, and the extra projection of the cabriole legs, demanding a certain spaciousness. For those who can accommodate them, there is much pleasure to be had from their flowing lines and the beautiful golden brown to which old walnut mellows. A characteristic shape is illustrated in Fig. 18, the outstanding features being the rounded cresting rail and seat, blending happily with the well-shaped leg, and the vase-shaped splat of the back, subtly curved to fit the human spine.

One of the attractions of antique furniture is the versatility of many of the pieces, and this is especially true of the Queen Anne writing- or dressing-table. It takes two forms, the first

FIG. 19

Basic shapes for English Furniture, early- to mid-eighteenth century

A. Kneehole writing- or dressing-table on cabriole legs.
B. Simple chest-of-drawers.
C. Chest-on-stand ('tallboy' or 'highboy') composed of table (A) used as a stand for chest (B).
D. Kneehole desk or dressing-table on bracket feet, with recessed cupboard; essentially a variation of the chest-of-drawers (B).

comprising a table-top with three drawers below—a shallow one at the centre flanked by two deeper ones—mounted on cabriole legs. If you take a good look at Fig. 19, you will see how this type of thing forms the stand of a tallboy, and also of a bureau. In the same way, a chest-of-drawers, mounted in various ways, takes on a variety of appearances. Furniture of this period was essentially simple in conception, relying on the permutations possible with a few basic shapes to produce a wide range of articles.

The second type of writing-table is really a chest-of-drawers with a kneehole provided. So as not to waste valuable space, a small cupboard is recessed in the kneehole (Fig. 19).

These chest-forms were supported on 'bracket' feet, which began to replace the 'bun' type of the William and Mary period at the beginning of the eighteenth century. They are extremely practical for holding heavy pieces a few inches off the floor, and are fairly easy to replace when necessary. This necessity does, inevitably, arise, and carefully replaced bracket feet are not, regarded as seriously depreciating the value of any but the rarest and most important pieces. (Fig. 17, F, G & H.)

These are the articles of outstandingly fine quality and beauty of design, prized by 'advanced' collectors, for whom this book does not pretend to cater, but such pieces provide a basis of comparison when we come down to earth and choose things of the same period, within our own price-range, and the opportunity to examine them, in shop or sale-room, private house or public museum, should never be missed. They are what remain to us of the output of the great craftsmen of that time, some of whom are known to us by name, but little of whose work can be identified.

There is comparatively little English furniture of any period that can be safely attributed to this or that maker. The custom of signing pieces—usual and, to some extent, obligatory in France—never took hold in Britain. Country craftsmen sometimes carved initials on chests and cupboards, but these were more often those of the owner rather than the maker of the piece. Very few London makers appended any kind of signature or trademark of a permanent nature to their work. From the late seventeenth century onwards, many of them stuck paper trade-labels on the backs of pieces, and on drawer-bottoms, but relatively few of them have remained attached to the articles. Sir

Ambrose Heal made a remarkable collection of these labels; an exhaustive study of them, and of pieces bearing them, was made a few years ago by Mr Ralph Edwards and Miss Margaret Jourdain, who published their findings in a work of the greatest interest and value to the keen student.[1] Great gaps still exist in the knowledge available, however. On the one hand, there is a great deal of anonymous work, and on the other, a list of craftsmen about whom little is known, in many cases, beyond their names and addresses. Relating the one to the other is not by any means easy, but it is possible, in a number of instances, to make reasonably safe attributions, supported by documentary evidence of one kind or another—labels, receipts, account-books, published designs and so on. Pieces of good quality that can be assigned in this way to a particular maker are sought after and usually sell at very much higher prices than do anonymous pieces of otherwise equal merit.

Not very long ago, I fondly imagined I had 'discovered' a piece in the bedroom of a Gloucestershire mansion, where there was to be an auction-sale. It was a bureau decorated in a curious manner supposed to be peculiar to Coxed and Woster, London cabinet-makers of the Queen Anne period, who specialized in the use of mulberry-wood veneers, inlaid with pewter stringing. Recognizing their style, I was almost sorry to find their trade-label stuck to the bottom of a drawer. There was now no chance of the thing being overlooked. Knowing I was thus in no position to buy it against competition from the big dealers, and thinking the piece of sufficient importance to merit a place in the national collection, I reported it, through a friend, to a retired official of the Victoria and Albert Museum. Much to the deflation of my ego, I was brusquely informed that my 'discovery' was well known to the powers-that-be, the ex-official himself having 'discovered' it some years before, and that the museum already had as much work by these makers as it could comfortably accommodate. I lamely left a bid of three hundred pounds, which was all I could afford to gamble, and was not surprised to learn the little bureau was subsequently 'knocked down' for three times that amount. As a consolation prize, I got a perfectly genuine marquetry chest-of-drawers, admittedly not so fine and bearing no fancy labels, but of the same period and in its way

[1] 'Georgian Cabinet Makers' (*Country Life*, 1944).

just as pleasing—for twenty-five pounds. That is the sort of difference that exists between the important and the unimportant.

George I (1714-1727). What is important to us, in attempting to grasp the fundamentals of the subject, is that while English furniture prior to 1700 is largely anonymous, with only one or two names like Grinling Gibbons and Daniel Marot to bandy about somewhat irrelevantly, from this time onwards it does become possible to describe many pieces according to the styles of individual craftsmen and designers. Unfortunately, it also becomes inevitable that these names should often be misapplied and misunderstood. One of the reasons for reading—and, indeed, for writing—a book like this is to reduce the incidence of such misapprehensions. The principle is that these names are used to describe pieces made in the manner we associate with this or that individual, not necessarily by him but by his contemporaries. A reproduction is also 'in the manner of', and care should be exercised in finding out exactly what is meant in each particular case. A 'Chippendale' chair, for example, might be a chair made by Chippendale, by another eighteenth-century maker, working to a Chippendale design, or a copy, faithful or otherwise, executed at any time during the last couple of hundred years. The use of these names is convenient. Sometimes it is just a little too convenient.

Many of the names exploited, legitimately or otherwise, are those of designers who never actually made furniture themselves. The first notable English architect to treat furniture-design as a serious part of his work was William Kent, whose inspiration largely derived from the grand Italian manner of Palladio. Kent's furniture was essentially architectural in conception, each piece being expressly intended to occupy a given position in a specific house. Some of his bookcases are of splendid proportions —veritable buildings in themselves—while his console tables, supported by carved caryatids—figures half-human, half-animal or architectural device—are magnificent if un-English in appearance. Much work of this kind was in carved *gesso*—a very hard plaster coating over a wood foundation—richly gilded. Such things were produced under Kent's direction, in the early Georgian period, for the statelier homes of England, and it is seldom that they settle down very happily in humbler surroundings. His designs are chiefly interesting as examples of the tremendous dignity to which the erstwhile restless and tormented Baroque manner could aspire under strict architectural discipline of the kind exerted by Palladio in Italy, Le Brun in France, Inigo Jones, Christopher Wren, and William Kent himself in Britain.

Quite distinct, in most ways, from this purely luxury-class was the usual run of early Georgian furniture, which carried on the best traditions of the short but important Queen Anne period, with the emphasis on good proportion, elegant lines to legs with the cabriole as the most usual shape, and rectilinear carcases. English craftsmen were slow to respond to the *Régence* influence, the *bombé* shape being little used in Britain, and at a later date, during the reign of George III. The nearest thing to it, at this time, was the so-called 'block front' which occurs, though rarely, in chests-of-drawers and bureau-bookcases. Here, the shaping is semi-serpentine but on the latitudinal plane only (see Fig. 21D). Examples of this shape occur in German and American furniture of the mid-eighteenth century, and authentic American examples are, very properly, highly prized. Some of them were doubtless shipped out from Europe, but American makers of importance were, by the beginning of the Georgian period, producing furniture every bit as good as European. (See p. 114.)

America was exporting to Britain some of the walnut which, during the reign of George I, remained the fashionable timber. The demand for it was such that there was not enough home-grown walnut to meet it, and supplies from the Continent gave out when a disease destroyed thousands of trees. Both 'black' and 'red' walnut from Virginia helped to make good the shortage, until a 'new' wood, first used about 1715 in Britain, became so popular that by the accession of George II in 1727, it had ousted walnut from favour. This latest novelty was an importation from Spanish possessions in the Caribbean, and was known as 'Spanish' mahogany.

George II (1727-1760). Early examples of mahogany furniture follow, basically, the designs employed over the previous quarter-century for walnut pieces, but certain modifications were immediately found to be necessary, since mahogany proved, at first, a difficult wood to work. These practical considerations, as much as changes in taste, accounted for some of the features of early to mid eighteenth-century work.

Although mahogany eventually came to be used, like walnut, in the form of veneers, most of the earlier work was executed in the solid, with a revival of interest in carving. Once the carvers had learned to temper their tools to suit the brittle quality of the wood, it proved a material reasonably well suited to sculpting the delicate scrolls and ribbon-work of the Rococo. Softer woods, such as pine, were used for the more fanciful mirror-frames and wall-brackets in the French manner, which were nearly always gilded, and beech was commonly employed for the frames of chairs and settees that were given this kind of finish.

Neither marquetry nor ormolu mounting were extensively used by the English at this period, and with a few important exceptions, the delicate extravagances of Louis XV *ébénistes* were avoided, in practice, by the London makers—though some of the designs which appeared were fantastic indeed. Many of them were never executed, so far as we know, in wood.

The most celebrated of the London design-books was Thomas Chippendale's *Gentleman and Cabinet Maker's Director*, the first edition of which was published in 1754, earning for its author an undying and, some think, undeserved fame. There is evidence that many of the designs were really the work of Lock and Copeland, who had published a Rococo pattern-book, under their own names, a few years earlier. But legend dies hard, and no matter what pedantic objections be raised, the bulk of mid-eighteenth-century English furniture always has been, and presumably always will be, loosely described as Chippendale. (Just how loosely is a matter I have already mentioned on p. 106). None of this proves Chippendale to be a charlatan. On the contrary, what we know of Chippendale's actual work suggests that he was a better cabinet-maker than the design-book suggests.

There are, for example, several *bombé* commodes in existence which can be attributed to him, decorated with the finest marquetry and rivalling the French cabinet-makers at their own game. These are among the important exceptions, previously mentioned, to the rule that most English work steers clear of this type of thing.

Exceptions, however, they remain, and though we are considering it, chronologically, under the general heading 'Baroque to Rococo', the bulk of mid-eighteenth century, medium-grade English furniture owes little to either of these continental styles, being either severely plain or relieved only very discreetly by a well-carved shell, a fretted ribbon or a fanciful brass handle. To this admirable class we will presently return, turning aside, for the moment, to consider English Rococo and also two styles that ran parallel with it—the so-called 'Chinese Chippendale' and 'Chippendale Gothic'. It should be borne in mind that, while

FIG. 20

English Rococo

A. Design for a 'claw table', after Ince and Mayhew, 1762.
B. Design for a chair, after Thomas Chippendale, 1754.
C. Design for a chair in Chippendale's manner, combining Gothic, Chinese and Rococo motifs, circa 1760.

all these styles originated in mid-century, during the reign of George II, they continued to be employed well into the next reign.

In their treatment of mirror-frames, overmantels and wall brackets, the English thoroughly enjoyed themselves with Rococo ornament. This is very obvious in a design-book published in 1762 by Ince and Mayhew, who were, to some extent, imitators of Chippendale. They were evidently determined to compete with the French on their own ground, as the text of the book is printed in both languages. I have attempted to reproduce one of their designs in Fig. 20A. This is one of three, described by them as 'Three very neat designs for Claw-Tables', and on the other side of the page, '*Trois Desseins élégans de Tables-à-un-seul-pied*'. I do not quite-see, myself, why a three-footed table should be shown balancing impossibly on two and be described, in French, as having only one. Tripod tables were made in large quantities at this time, in all grades, as it was the fashion to throw tea-parties for as many as a couple of hundred guests. I have read that, to meet such social demands, as many as fifty of these tables were regarded as part of the normal furnishing of a London house, but I must say I find it difficult to believe. Chippendale omits them entirely from the *Director*.

To what extent they succeeded, we do not know, but Messrs Ince and Mayhew make it clear that they hoped to do a two-way traffic, importing French furniture and exporting English.

To prove that the British could out-rock the Rococo if they really wanted to, Robert Manwaring produced, three years later, in 1765, some designs for 'rural' chairs which employ the asymmetrical shapes of tree-branches for the frames. Quite mad.

If we consider the designs published under Chippendale's name, we find ourselves rather nearer to reality. A great many pieces survive which bear a fairly strong resemblance to these engravings, but this cannot be accepted as evidence that they are his work, or that of his employees (he is supposed to have employed about twenty-two craftsmen), since his book was intended for, and was bought by, his colleagues in the trade. Anyone able to scrape together the requisite forty-eight shillings could buy a copy, and use it as a pattern-book, making modifications to suit himself. Two pounds eight shillings—about seven dollars—was a lot of money two hundred years ago; indeed, in these days of paper-backs and masses of free trade-catalogues, it still seems a high price for a book which was undoubtedly meant, at least in part, to advertise Chippendale's business. The fact that it ran into three editions suggests that the boys thought it pretty good value.

Figure 20B is taken from a design in the 1754 edition. It is typical of a great variety of mid-eighteenth-century chairs in the Rococo manner, the back having a 'camel' hump and delicately pierced splat. Chair-backs were often much more elaborate, as in the case of ribbon—or as they were then called, 'ribband'—backed specimens. The leg here is an elegant, very French version of the cabriole, terminating in a neat, upward-curling scroll. Various kinds of foot are found on chairs of the period, the claw-and-ball being met with frequently.

Reproductions of Chippendale's Rococo style are legion. Some of them are now a respectable age, and of excellent quality. Some of the ribbon-back chairs made about 1880 are good enough to command prices in the region of $450 to $600 for a set of six side-chairs and two elbow-chairs.

Frame settees—i.e. those with upholstery on the seat only—follow chair-design exactly, being built on the usual eighteenth-century principle of linking two, three or four chair-backs together.

Both Chippendale's book and that of Ince and Mayhew illustrate pieces of the kind known as 'Chinese Chippendale', and the latter even suggest 'japanning' as the most suitable finish for some. In the main, however, the *chinoiseries* of this period were not lacquered, as they had been in earlier times, but relied on shape, together with fretted and carved ornament, to achieve their rather strange purpose. Few *trained* observers had ever visited China, and no authentic report appeared until 1757 —three years after the publication of the first edition of the *Director*—when Sir William Chambers, architect to George III a few years later, and the first English member of his profession to visit the country, brought out his Designs for *Chinese Buildings, Furniture, Dresses, Etc*. He was not, personally, in sympathy with the craze for pseudo-oriental styles, and intended his book to be a corrective measure against the more fantastic conceptions of the East that were prevalent. When Chippendale produced his designs for furniture 'in the Chinese taste', he did not have the benefit of Chambers' book, or any other reliable information, to work on. Ince and Mayhew presumably had the advantage of studying the work of Chambers before getting out the drawings for their *Universal System of Household Furniture*, but their ideas seem much more in keeping with the popular conception than with the authentic report.

When Thomas Chippendale, Yorkshireman, set himself to please fashionable fancy for exotic styles, the results were curious—sometimes charming, sometimes hideous. Chairs in this oriental manner usually had square-framed backs set with geometric frets, and straight, square legs carved to match. Torchère stands for candelabra and small tables with carefully fretted galleries are among the more attractive examples of 'Chinese Chippendale' which can take their place in the small house. Some remarkable cabinets and wall-shelves, with pagoda-shaped tops, still serve admirably the purpose for which they were intended—the display of porcelain. Some very good, small examples are to be had, but they tend to be expensive. Large versions of the cabinets are to be found in the 'break-front' form: a centre section projecting a couple of inches beyond the side-pieces flanking it. This was a characteristic, and very pleasing, method of constructing bookcases and cabinets at that period. The 'Chinese Chippendale' interpretation, however, is sometimes rather much to bear. Each of the three sections has its pagoda-top, from which temple-bells of carved mahogany hang, and in place of the cupboard-section below, which break-front bookcases usually have, there is a stand of square legs that always seems to me too frail for the carcase above. Several that I have seen, based on designs in *The Universal System*, appear to have been made at a rather later date, probably during the period of revived interest in *chinoiserie* that came in the Regency, about 1815.

Even in its heyday, during the 1750's and 60's, not everyone accepted the Rococo and its oriental off-shoot. Horace Walpole heartily disapproved, preferring the odd, peculiarly English, revival of the Gothic style, so long despised (see p. 22). Fellow enthusiasts built houses complete with towers, spires, battlements, pointed arches, gargoyles and tracery, and some even went so far as to construct 'ruins' and romantic grottos in their landscaped gardens. It was, in fact, the beginning of the Romantic movement, which lasted until the late nineteenth century. Its later phases will be discussed in Chapter Six.

This first outbreak, in the middle of the eighteenth century, was catered for by the furniture-makers, and the resulting products are known as '*Chippendale Gothic*'. There was no attempt to reproduce early oak pieces. Most of the furniture in this manner was constructed of mahogany, and followed the usual shapes of the time, employing cusped arches and other Gothic ornament where, in other models, Rococo or Chinese motifs would have appeared. Indeed, so closely do all these styles run together that it is not at all unusual to find them overlapping, with pointed arches, C-scrolls and oriental lattice-work mixed up together in the same piece. Odd and alarming though this must sound, the result is often very pleasing. (See Fig. 20c.)

Like the 'Chinese Chippendale', the legs of 'Chippendale Gothic' furniture are vertical, often formed by a cluster of four columns, and represent an important break-away from the cabriole—the curving line of the Rococo which Hogarth regarded as the first essential to beauty. It is significant, too, that both these fanciful styles draw their inspiration from architecture, and though Gothic arch and Chinese pagoda may seem a far remove from Greek frieze, they are symptomatic of a paradoxical desire to discard the frills of the Rococo in favour of a more architectural style, without submitting completely to classical discipline. It was a mood that was basically affecting French as well as English design, and before proceeding with the effect on British furniture, it would be as well to look across the Channel once more. But first, we must look across the ocean, to observe the manifestations of the Rococo movement in America.

America (*Colonial Period*)

From about 1700 onwards, an ever-increasing consciousness of the need for comfort and beauty influenced the furnishing of the more well-to-do American home. As in Europe, the humbler folk continued to make or have made for them simple pieces of solid joinery, but those who could afford to do so set out to emulate London fashions. The cabriole leg arrived rather late, turned types being general until about 1720, but from then on, the cabriole remained a firm favourite for some seventy years.

English influence was dominant, many homes being furnished

very largely with pieces ordered in London. This is especially true of the planters' houses in the South. Elsewhere, a native tradition developed, and as I remarked earlier, some of the work was of the highest order, and possessed a flavour of its own. Block-fronted chests, bureaux and bureau-bookcases, mentioned on p. 107, were the speciality of John Goddard of Newport, Rhode Island, who was fond of decorating such pieces with the shell motif carved on an unusually large scale. Another important centre was Philadelphia, where William Savery, Thomas Affleck and Benjamin Randolph all produced furniture of outstanding quality. Savery worked during the second quarter of the eighteenth century, making well-shaped pieces in the Queen Anne and Early Georgian manner. Affleck and Randolph, during the third quarter, worked in Chippendale's Rococo manner, and both seem to have been devoted to the claw-and-ball foot. New York, Boston and the Connecticut Valley can all boast a respectable history of cabinet-making dating from this period.

CHAPTER FIVE

Rococo to Neo-Classic

IN 1754, the year that saw the appearance in England of Chippendale's *Director*, a Frenchman, Cochin, wrote his *Supplication to Goldsmiths, Bronze-Chasers and Wood-Carvers*, in which he begs the carvers to realize that it is ruinously expensive to cut good, straight timber into elaborate, sinuous shapes. His protest was symptomatic of the time. The French were getting rather bored with the Rococo, just at the time when it was at the height of its popularity in Britain. Even there, Walpole was grumbling.

France

   Transitional Period (1755-1770). During the latter years of Louis XV's reign, there was a gradual shedding of Rococo ornament in favour of 'Greek', as it was called. All over Europe there was a renewed interest in classical architecture, stimulated by the excavations at Pompeii and Herculaneum. At first it was ornament and ornament only that reflected the change. Ormolu mounts took on severe classical forms, in place of the C-scrolls of the *rocaille*, but the cabriole leg remained in favour, and was just about the last Rococo element to go. Cochin's *cri du coeur* went unheeded, so far as wasting timber on curving legs was concerned. But ten years after he had uttered it, carcase shapes, at any rate, had become rectilinear in place of the *bombé* form, so that when Mme de Pompadour died in 1764, the transition to a more severe style was almost complete. When her successor, du Barry, furnished the Château de Louveciennes in 1770, it was in the style we call Louis XVI, although Louis XV lived for another four years. It is an odd fact that the styles we call by the names of English monarchs usually outlast their name-sakes, whereas the kings of France tended to last longer than the manner of decoration named after them.

   Louis XVI (1770-1790). These dates are the effective ones so far as 'style Louis XVI' is concerned. In fact, Louis XVI succeeded his grandfather in 1774 and was executed in 1792. He was a good and kind man, middle-class rather than aristocratic in his outlook, with a genuine respect for fine craftsmanship, who could have earned a decent living as a locksmith. Marie-Antoinette was a pleasure-loving beauty who delighted in beautiful things. Neither of them, unhappily, had the strength of character to save their thrones, or their heads, from the excesses of the inevitable revolution but, at least while they lived, the arts and crafts continued to enjoy royal patronage, and the furniture of this period must be acknowledged to be unsurpassed for perfection of proportion, purity of line, discretion in decoration, functional suitability and quality in execution.

Once it had emerged from the transitional phàse, the style may be said to be based on straight lines rather than curves, and the atmosphere it engenders is one of formal grace as distinct from the frivolous elegance of the preceding reign. Carcase-shapes become rectangular, legs vertical—usually round in section, and delicately tapering towards the toe, the stem fluted either straight down or spirally. The feet of such pieces as commodes are sometimes of square section, but these, too, are tapered. Drawers are often edged with a plain brass moulding, and ormolu mounts are in the form of acanthus leaves, laurel wreaths, human and animal heads, and other classical motifs. Marquetry becomes more restrained, tending to formal, all-over designs, such as *'marqueterie à la reine'*—tiny flowers within a trellis-work—used on pieces made for Marie-Antoinette and, of course, for others too. Parquetry was an even more formalized variant, employing small pieces of geometrically cut veneers to build up a mosaic which has an uncannily three-dimensional effect.

In some ways, Louis XVI designs recall those of Louis XIV, in that they mark a return to architectural form and classical mannerisms, but the way in which they are employed is essentially different, with emphasis on lightness and grace, as opposed to heaviness and pomposity. Certain techniques of the earlier period were also revived, such as Boulle-work (see p. 44), which had been out of fashion during the Rococo phase. Porcelain plaques from the Royal Porcelain Factory at Sèvres were inset into the doors of cabinets and the friezes of tables.

Chairs, in particular, contrast sharply with those of Louis XV period. Gone are the sinuous curves, and in their place we find pure geometry—backs that are square, oval or chastely arched in the case of upholstered items, backs composed of deceptively simple-looking lyre-shapes for the lighter type of chair. Arms, when present, have their supports set well forward, rising naturally above the leg, instead of sweeping backwards in a flourishing curve, as they were wont to do at mid-century. Chair- and settee-frames were almost invariably painted or gilded, but some were of solid mahogany. It is worth noting that chair-legs veneered with cross-banded kingwood, which one sometimes sees on furniture of excellent quality, indicate a nineteenth-century origin. This technique was employed on table-legs in the eighteenth century, but not on chairs and settees.

On the whole, the *Louis Seize* period saw a reduction in the variety of types, which had been tending to multiply alarmingly with every requirement, logical and illogical, being met with a specialized article of furniture. However, most of the more popular items of the *Louis Quinze* period continued to be produced, with modifications in design and decoration to suit the new mode, and some of them were, in form, more typical of the later reign. In particular, this is true of the *chiffonier*. This term often leads to some confusion. It comes from the word *chiffon*—literally, a rag, but used colloquially to mean any small, female garment. A *chiffonnier* (with two N's) was a rag-picker, and the feminine form, *chiffonnière*, was that which was first applied to a piece of furniture used as a repository for women's clothes. (Even today, the women's dress industry is referred to, idiomatically, as 'the rag trade', while chiffon has come to mean a particular kind of flimsy textile.) The spelling was modified, both in Britain and France, to *chiffonier*, but came to mean rather different things. In England, after 1800, it was a small sideboard, with one drawer and a cupboard below, and a shelf fitted above. In France, in the late eighteenth century, it was a tall, narrow chest of drawers, rather like a tallboy but constructed in one piece, not two. The nearest English equivalent is the so-called 'Wellington' chest of the nineteenth century. The number of drawers in a *chiffonier* varies from six to eight. Seven was a popular average, and the seven-drawer *chiffonier* is often called a *semainier*, as it has one for every day of the week.

Bedside-tables were among the things on which much care was lavished. They are sometimes known by the charming description '*en cas*'. 'Just in case', they were fitted out, not only as 'necessary cabinets', but as supper-tables. All sorts of emergencies might arise in the middle of the night, and Paris being then, as now, Paris, no doubt they often did. Frenchmen believed in having just about everything needed for their physical well-being close-to-hand, not omitting a bite to eat. These days, people go to bed with their ulcers, and keep a glass of milk on the bedside table. Just in case.

The desk and *bonheur-du-jour* continued as great favourites, the cylinder-top being developed late in the Louis XV reign and becoming a popular feature in that of Louis XVI. The best-known example is that begun by Oeben and finished by his pupil, Riesener (see p. 86).

Riesener seems to have been a singularly fortunate man. He succeeded to his late master's business, became cabinet-maker to the king in his place, and married the Widow Oeben. Unlike so many servants of the royal family, he survived the Revolution and died a rich man. Certainly, he was a wonderful craftsman who deserved to succeed.

Franco-German

Indeed, he is regarded by some experts as the greatest of the eighteenth-century cabinet-makers of France, with David Röntgen a close second. Both of them were German by birth, and perhaps for patriotic reasons, some shrewd Frenchmen give pride of place to cabinet-makers with French names, such as Dubois, Migeon, Blanchard, Meunier, Dupin, Brizard, Tilliard, Séné . . . The list could be extended indefinitely, as masterpeices signed by all these and many more survive. The fact remains that several of the really great men—acknowledged geniuses in their own day—among the Paris cabinet-makers were German by birth, and the high peak of 'French' furniture owes much to their skill and ingenuity. Oeben, Riesener and Röntgen were appointed cabinet-makers to the royal family, and among their fellow countrymen were Weisweiler and Canabas. There were many others who emigrated to France and made their homes there, investing the natural grace of the French product with the constructive skill of German ingenuity. Such pieces as toilet-tables, writing-tables, and music-stands with cleverly concealed drawers, adjustable shelves, folding mirrors and other compli-cated mechanical devices were very often features of this Franco-German work, one Peter Kinzing being the inventor of many tricksy pieces.

In the last chapter, I mentioned the importance of the German cabinet-makers, and it may seem I am excessively anxious to stress it. In a way, I am, not because I am more pro-German than pro-French, but because credit should be given where it is due, and it does seem to me that, in this context, the 'Frenchness' of French furniture is sometimes a little exaggerated. David Röntgen was the son of a famous German cabinet-maker, Abraham Röntgen, whose ivory-inlaid furniture was highly prized by the German nobility. David Röntgen, while he was cabinet-maker to the Queen of France, from 1780 until the Revolution, was also a member of the Paris guild. In his Paris establishment he kept large stocks of furniture which had actually been manufactured at Neuwied, near Coblenz. From this stock he supplied all comers, including the Empress of Russia. When we speak of 'Louis XVI' furniture, we are really talking about a cosmopolitan, pan-European style, centred on Paris but having international ramifications both in regard to its manufacture and its outlet.

Britain

Britain was perhaps more inclined to go its own way than were the other European countries, but influences passed to and fro across the Channel. Röntgen himself, before surrendering completely to the Neo-Classic style, imitated Chippendale's Rococo manner in Germany—a style which the English had themselves picked up from French originals, devised largely by an Italian! The late eighteenth century is often made out to be a relatively easy period to understand in terms of national differences, but it will be appreciated, from the foregoing, that the truth is rather more complex than superficial appearances might suggest.

The version of the Rococo evolved by Chippendale and his contemporaries and which served as a model for Röntgen, was described in the last chapter, together with its curious cousins, 'Chippendale Gothic' and 'Chinese Chippendale'. About 1760, there was a lessening of interest in these more exotic styles, due partly to a general preference for something plainer, and partly to that same admiration for classical design which was inspiring continental craftsmen. This first expressed itself in a reduction of scrolled shapes. Though the cabriole leg was certainly not abandoned, it was replaced, to a very large extent, by a straight, square leg, often relieved only by a chamfer on the inside corner. Chair-legs, in particular, were made in this way, the backs of dining chairs being simplified versions of the elaborately fretted Rococo types. A comfortable arm-chair of the period was the 'Gainsborough' or 'Raeburn', with padded back, open arms and low seat on square legs.

Sideboards—which, in the *Director*, are simply side-tables with no drawers or cupboards—also have these severe, square legs, with a small bracket, curved and purely ornamental, breaking the right-angle where the leg joins the frieze.

Furniture of this transitional period, which has discarded the flourishes of the Rococo and has not yet adopted the mannerisms of the Neo-Classic to any marked extent, makes up a very large class of English work that is of the greatest interest to the modest collector. I call it, for the want of a better name, 'English Chippendale'—but I must hasten to add that this is not an official designation that you will find elsewhere. I find it a convenient term—in my own mind, rather than in conversation—for the plainer pieces made in the third quarter of the eighteenth century, of which sufficient survive, in varying grades, for them to be available to anyone who can afford to buy anything at all, old or new, worth calling furniture.

For the man with some money to spend, there is the first-class, London-made piece; for those less well-off, the work of the provincial makers, not quite so refined, but still achieving a high standard; for the really hard-up, who would otherwise be mortgaging their earnings for the next few years on gimcrack junk bought on the hire-purchase system, there is the category called 'country' or 'farmhouse' Chippendale, of honest oak, ash, beech and elm which quaintly emulates the sophisticated city styles. (See Chapter Seven.)

Of the leading London makers, many are known by name, but there is little furniture that can be definitely attributed to this or that maker (see p. 104). Nor do we have much information about them as men. Manwaring, Ince, Mayhew, and Chippendale himself have already been mentioned. Haig, his partner, remains a shadowy figure. William Vile and John Cobb emerge a little more distinctly. They were more highly thought of, in their own day, than was Thomas Chippendale himself, and were appointed cabinet-makers to George III. For this reason, some of their work is fully documented, and their style is sometimes recognizable—especially their magnificent, architecturally conceived bookcases. Of George Hepplewhite we shall speak presently.

Most of these had their headquarters in the vicinity of St Martin's Lane. I was once shown the premises which Chippendale occupied. Allowing for structural alterations, they didn't seem very big, and it is quite possible that this address was for prestige purposes as much as anything else. He may have retained other workshops elsewhere—perhaps in Long Acre, which was his address before the move to St Martin's Lane. Doubtless much work of a basic sort, and some of a highly specialized kind, would have been farmed out to lesser lights.

The most favoured wood, prior to the introduction of satin-wood, was mahogany. It was used both in the solid and in the form of finely figured veneers. Veneering was usually executed on a pine foundation, with oak for drawer-sides and bottoms. Most jointing was of the dove-tail or mortice-and-tenon varieties. Chair-frames were jointed up with dowel-joints by French craftsmen at this period, the rail usually being joined to the leg with three dowel-pins. This practice began to be widely practised in England in the early nineteenth century, and is still extensively used.

French polishing, so-called, was another technique not yet developed. In the eighteenth century, various recipes for polishing were employed. Many people are shocked when told that Chippendale advocated the use of varnish to fill the grain. This was then rubbed down with powdered pumice or brick-dust. The wood was fed with a little linseed oil, and a fine finish obtained with beeswax, strenuously applied.

Pieces characteristic of this plain, English type of furniture were chests-of-drawers of varying sizes—three feet six inches is the standard. Anything smaller is rarer, more attractive to look at and easier to utilize in small modern houses, and therefore commands a higher price. A pleasing feature on some of mid-eighteenth-century vintage is a variant of the bracket foot, called an 'ogee' foot (Fig. 21E). This provides an S-shaped curve in the solid. If you like throwing Latin tags around, you can call it *cyma recta*. It was suited only to carcases built on a right-angled plan, and was discarded in favour of a splayed, tapered foot on

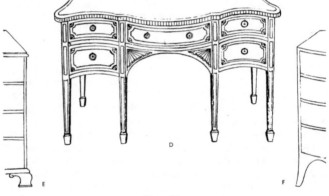

Fig. 21

The Return to Discipline

A. Chippendale chair on square legs with ladder-back, circa 1760.
B. Hepplewhite chair showing Adam's influence: on square-tapered legs with shield-shaped back, employing Prince of Wales' feathers as a motif, circa 1780.
C. Sheraton Chair on turned, tapered legs, with rounded seat, the back of rectangular outline. This also employs the Prince of Wales' feathers in lighter form. Circa 1795.
D. Hepplewhite sideboard incorporating drawers and cupboards disguised as drawers, with shaped front and square-tapered legs ending in spade feet, circa 1785.
E. Detail of chest-of-drawers with bracket foot of 'ogee' form, circa 1770 to 1790.
F. Detail of bow-fronted chest-of-drawers with splayed foot, circa 1770 to 1820.

the introduction of serpentine and bow-fronted shapes, which were types distinctive of the gradually emerging Neo-Classic style. (See Fig. 21F.)

They are usually associated with the name of Hepplewhite, but that does not mean, of course, that he had any copyright. Most of the makers, including those already referred to by name, followed the general trend of fashion. Just as certain styles are known as 'Chippendale' because they are found in his book, so others are known as 'Hepplewhite' because prototypes appear in his designs, published under the title *Cabinet-Maker and Upholsterers' Guide* in 1788, when he was already dead and gone. He had died two years before, and his widow, Alice, carried on the business in the name of A. Hepplewhite and Co. It was she who brought out the book, and immortalized her husband's name. He does not seem to have been very well-known in his own lifetime.

The designs of Hepplewhite are extremely pleasing and very practical. They present the Neo-Classic style in a way that suited then, and still suits today, English and American taste. But Hepplewhite did not create the style, and neither did Alice. If any man was responsible for it, that man was Robert Adam, architect, aided by his brother James.

Adam returned from an extensive tour of Europe, which had included a special study of Roman architecture, in 1758. No doubt he had also gleaned much from the continental designers, who were beginning to respond to the enthusiasm of amateur scholars for the formal beauty of classical design.

Certainly, Robert Adam was fired with this enthusiasm himself, and once back in Britain, proceeded to design whole streets of houses and, if he possibly could, everything in them, according to the Neo-Classic principles, based on the 'orders' of architecture, and the correct use of column and entablature, decorated only with appropriate ornament.

Many of the leading furniture-makers of the day worked under his direction, including Chippendale and Hepplewhite. Frankly, I never quite know how to distinguish 'Adam' furniture from 'Hepplewhite'. To me, Hepplewhite is simply a name that is conveniently applied to furniture executed according to the principles of Adam. Perhaps it is reasonable to distinguish between the obviously architecturally designed pieces, calling them 'Adam', and those of the run-of-the-mill, cabinet-maker's-stock-item kind, which can be termed 'Hepplewhite'. A number of pieces of furniture—particularly side-tables of an ornamental nature, and stands for urns and candelabra—appear in Adam's published designs, *Works in Architecture*, which came out in 1778, and anything closely resembling them can fairly be described as 'Adam'. Hepplewhite's *Guide* did not present itself for another ten years. In it, we find most of the features which are associated with Adam's style, incorporated in furniture of a rather less pretentious sort. Adam designed exclusively for great houses. Hepplewhite translated these designs, adapted them and added to them, in a way that made them available to a much wider public.

In the same year as his designs appeared, posthumously, the *Cabinet-Makers' London Book of Prices* was published, in which several pieces attributed to Hepplewhite are illustrated. This book was mainly the work of Thomas Shearer, who also issued, in the same year, his *Designs for Household Furniture*—largely a duplication of his own contribution to the former work.

Between 1791 and 1794, another great name emerges. Thomas Sheraton, journeyman cabinet-maker from Stockton-on-Tees, had set himself up some years before in Soho as drawing-master, designer and author. Although there must surely be pieces of furniture in existence that were made by him, there is not a single one that can definitely be attributed to him as the actual maker, and so far as we know, he had no workshops in London. The chances are, therefore, that any extant examples of his craftsmanship are still residing, incognito, in the provinces —perhaps in the faded drawing-room of a country mansion, or the back-bedroom of a North Country boarding house. You might even be the only person in the world to own a piece made by Sheraton himself.

In his *Cabinet-Maker's and Upholsterer's Drawing Book*, which appeared in four parts, he presents 113 plates, all of them designs which rely almost entirely on the Neo-Classic style introduced by Adam and developed by Hepplewhite, Shearer, and others. To a large extent, they reflect the taste of the day, and summarize for us the development of the style in England between 1760 and 1795. But Sheraton was no mere copyist, and as we shall presently see, some of his work was an original contribution.

If it is difficult to discriminate between Adam and Hepplewhite, it is also sometimes very hard to draw a dividing line between their work and that of Sheraton. For example, it is customary to describe chairs with oval and shield-shaped backs as Hepplewhite, but these shapes were favoured by Adam and Sheraton too.

One can concern one's self unduly about the naming of a design. Until a great deal of furniture has been studied and compared with original eighteenth-century designs, it is far more sensible and practical to think of the late-eighteenth century period as a whole—a movement away from the florid Rococo and towards the severe lines of the Neo-Classic. If I use the name of this or that designer to describe a particular manner, throughout the remainder of this chapter, it is with the proviso that the application is a somewhat loose one.

The discarding of the cabriole leg in favour of a straight square one has already been mentioned. This came about shortly after the middle of the century, and was in general use in the 1760's, in association with chair-backs very like those shown in Fig. 20A. The next step was the tapering of the leg, still employing a square section, but abandoning the chamfer on the inside corner. Square-taper legs sometimes continue uninterruptedly to the floor, and sometimes finish in a neat, spade-shaped foot. Tapered legs of circular section, finely fluted, are less common. Both styles were used on tables, chairs, cabinets and all pieces raised from the ground. Chair backs were fundamentally altered—oval, shield, heart, and square shaped being the most satisfactory. These were upholstered in the case of arm-chairs, the wooden frame being exposed, and usually left open for side-chairs, the space being partly occupied by a delicate construction, not solid enough to be called a splat, although that is the technical term for it. This took various forms, but the basic principle involves the use of verticals, straight or curved, set close together and usually employing one or other of the favourite classical motifs as a central feature, linking them together.

The repertoire of these ornaments is extensive. Those most usually encountered are the 'Adam's' urn, the wheat-sheaf, the Prince of Wales' feathers, the heads of rams and lions (these were more often employed in metal-work than in wood), pendant husks, swags of drapery, and musical instruments. Adam was fond of employing the classical column, but in slender form. One of his great achievements was a revival of pure, classical styles without the heaviness of the early eighteenth century, Palladian manner of William Kent.

These ornaments were carved, painted or inlaid. Adam favoured the decorating of furniture by skilled artists in marquetry and paint. Chippendale produced some of his finest pieces under his influence. The brilliant woman-painter, Angelica Kauffmann, was employed by the Adam brothers to paint mythological subjects on elegant pieces of satinwood. This began to be imported from the West Indies about 1760, and a little later from the East Indies. After the discovery of Australia, more was brought to Britain from there.

Painted satinwood is very charming—a wonderful golden colour which sets off the pigments to perfection. Good, early pieces are difficult to find and can be very expensive. There was a revival of its use in Edwardian times, and some of this late work is of excellent quality and not at all to be despised.

The use of satinwood was mostly confined to drawing-room and bedroom furniture, but it did sometimes appear in the dining-room. It was extensively used for marquetry-work in a mahogany ground. A typical example is the oval of satinwood which surrounds the shell inlaid into so much 'Sheraton' furniture. Incidentally, although delicately inlaid furniture of this period is nearly always labelled 'Sheraton', Thomas himself rejected it as old-fashioned and expensive. He preferred painted decoration.

Quite a lot of furniture was completely painted. Popular colours were white and green, picked out in gold. Adam's earlier style also include pieces elaborately carved and gilded all over.

Beech was the wood most usually used for furniture intended to be entirely coated with paint or gilt. It was also used as a cheaper substitute for satinwood, especially for legs. It is a good, close-grained timber, but very prone to attack by wood-worm. In the late eighteenth and early nineteenth centuries, it was a general practice to construct the frame of chair-seats in beech, and veneer them with mahogany. Mahogany was still expensive, although the heavy duty formerly imposed on its importation had been mitigated in 1747. This economizing on seat-frames has had unfortunate results for us today. Mahogany is not much liked by wood-worm. They don't seem to care for the taste, preferring a savoury morsel of walnut, elm, oak, pine or beech. The result is that a great number of otherwise sound chairs are wormed in the beech seat-rails, but it is foolish to turn down a good set because of this disadvantage. The worm can be treated or, if it really is too bad, the rails can usually be carefully replaced, using the original veneer.

Mahogany, relieved with discreet carving or marquetry, remained the most popular wood for furniture that combined elegance with practicability, at least until 1800. Satinwood and gilt were all very well for the women in the drawing-room, but the men preferred the dining-room furnished in a wood nearer the colour of their red wine. I remarked earlier that furniture can be divided into masculine and feminine, and I think the principle especially applies to late eighteenth-century work. Sheraton's designs, especially, veer towards the feminine, and so do Adam's. Hepplewhite's, although his widow had a hand in their publication, manage to remain more masculine, but at the same time elegant.

For all its grace, the sort of dining-room furniture associated with Hepplewhite's name has a fine male tang about it. He is usually credited with the invention of a side-board with built-in cupboards and drawers, as distinct from the Chippendale and early Adam versions, which consisted of a plain side-table flanked by separate pedestal-cupboards. The Hepplewhite side-board is especially suitable for use in a small home. It stands on square-taper legs, has one or two drawers at the centre, a cupboard on one side and a deep drawer, usually compartmented and lined with lead for use as a cellarette, on the other. It's shape, like so much carcase furniture of the period, is often serpentine or bow-fronted. The *bombé* swell had never been popular in Britain, but the bow and serpentine curves, requiring shaping on the latitudinal plane only, were very popular from about 1770 onwards. The bow shape was less expensive to produce, and was consequently much more common. Heavier versions of both bow and serpentine sideboards, chests, etc., continued to be made well into the nineteenth century.

The dining table of the period takes one of two principle forms, both of which allow for expansion and contraction of size. The earlier of the two consists of a centre-section in the form of a table with flaps, which can be further extended by placing a 'D'-end or half-circular table at each end. The legs are uniformly square on the earlier examples, square-tapered on the later. The advantage of such a table for a small house is that it can be split up into its component parts, all of which are complete items of furniture in themselves.

The other type was the two- or three-pillar table, which consists of a pair of end pieces mounted on tripod pedestals (centre-columns with three feet splaying out from each), and a leaf, supported on slides, to go between the two. Three-pillar tables have a centre-section similar to the end-pieces, except that it usually has four feet, and are supplied with two leaves for insertion, one each side of the centre-section.

For the very small dining-room, or the home which has a multi-purpose living-room, the late Georgian breakfast table is adequate and pleasing. This is a single-pedestal table, having three or four splayed feet, with brass toe-pieces, incorporating casters. The top is either oval or rectangular with rounded corners, and the better quality examples are cross-banded. The top is hinged to the base, and held in position by a spring clip, so that it can be tipped to a vertical position. This, combined with the mobility provided by the casters, make it very easy to move out of the way for cleaning the carpet, not to mention the occasions when this has to be taken up for the younger members of the family to dance.

Some very useful and attractive case-furniture was made in the George III period—bookcases, bureau-bookcases, china-display cabinets, and corner cabinets. With these, we may consider the 'blind front' bureau bookcase, the chest-of-drawers and the 'gentlemen's' wardrobe. Although all these things sound so dissimilar, they are in fact related, in the same way that such things were related in the time of Queen Anne and George I. Basically, we have a chest-of-drawers and a case with either a wooden door or one which is glazed with small panels of glass, set into narrow mouldings (astrigals) arranged in many fanciful designs. (An arrangement of thirteen was popular, and has given rise to the fallacy that corner cabinets, if genuine, must have thirteen panes. This is nonsense.) It will be seen from Fig. 22 that various combinations of these basic forms provide a very large variety of useful furniture.

FIG. 22

Basic forms for English Carcase Furniture, 1775 to 1800

A. Bureau-bookcase with glazed doors.
B. China-cabinet with glazed doors.
C. Oval brass handle, typical of the classical style.
D. Corner-cabinet with glazed doors.
E. Gentleman's wardrobe with oval panels to the doors.
F. Breakfront-bookcase with glazed doors.
(Note that all these pieces employ the same basic forms in various
        combinations, to provide a wide range of articles)

Equally useful were the many dainty pieces—folding card tables, sewing tables, Pembroke tables with short flaps supported by brackets, which Sheraton especially delighted in devising, often introducing novelties in the way of mechanical contrivances a little on the lines of *Louis Seize* pieces designed by the Franco-German, Peter Kinzing, but nevertheless having sufficient originality to justify Sheraton's fame. He earned his place in the history of fine furniture, and was poorly rewarded for it in his own life-time. In 1803, he produced another book, the *Cabinet Dictionary*, in which he tries, rather desperately, to keep up with the latest trends towards an even more exaggerated, and rather different, version of the Neo-Classic, which we shall deal with in the next chapter. He died, aged fifty-five, in 1806—very poor and a little mad.

America

The interpretation of the Neo-Classic style in America was much nearer to English than to French originals. The outstanding exponent was Duncan Phyfe of New York, other well-known makers being John Seymour & Son of Boston, Samuel McIntire of Salem, Matthew Edgerton of New Jersey. Phyfe is best known for his skilful deployment of the lyre-form for chair-backs and the arms of sofas. The small side-board was one of the things which American makers made especially well. Edgerton is reputedly the maker of a particular serpentine-fronted type having an unusual cupboard at the centre, below the drawers, in place of the knee-hole-like arrangement common in Britain. McIntire produced some fine shield-back chairs in the Hepplewhite manner, while John and James Seymour specialized in an interesting type of writing desk, modelled closely on the Louis XVI *bonheur-du-jour*, usually fitted with tambour doors; was this, perhaps, the forerunner of the American roll-top desk?

Probably not. A great deal of present-day office-type furniture, including the swivel chair, seems to owe its origins to the American religious sect, known as the 'Shakers', who made their own furniture in the late eighteenth and early nineteenth centuries. They were very strict in their observances, and forbade the use of brass handles on furniture as vain and sinful. It may well be that the use of wooden knobs on much British furniture of country make stems from a conscious or unconscious sense of 'sin'. Many of the country people, especially in Wales, were Nonconformists of one kind or another, who inherited the Puritan tradition.

Much eighteenth-century furniture was fitted with brass handles originally, some of which have inevitably been lost or damaged over the years. Reproduction replacements are the answer, and nothing to be ashamed of; but if you can find a piece with the original brasses, it really is worth paying a little more. The keen collector is ready to pay quite a lot more. A good dealer will always tell you whether the handles are original or not, and point out any other repairs of which he is aware.

There is, fortunately, a great deal of good furniture of this period surviving, especially in Britain, and the most conservative minded, with a taste for severe, undecorated furniture, can always find something of the late eighteenth century to suit his purpose and his pocket. But the supply is drying up. There is only a certain amount to go round, the demand steadily increases and in a few more years it will be as difficult to find a good, plain Georgian chest-of-drawers as it now is to acquire a fine *Lou Seize* commode.

'Gather ye rosebuds while ye may . . .'

CHAPTER SIX

Neo-Classic to Romantic

To divide the nineteenth century into two periods—'Regency' and 'Victorian'—and leave it at that is a convenient but misleading simplification. There was nothing like so clear a dividing line between the end of the one and the beginning of the other as is sometimes supposed, and to understand the furniture made between 1800 and 1900—even that made in England alone—it is necessary to take into account historical developments in Europe generally, particularly in late eighteenth-century France.

France
Directoire and Empire (1790–1815). The leaders of the French Revolution were not content to overthrow the monarchy and decimate the aristocracy. They sought to disparage the whole way of life, and its very background, that had been adopted by the court of Louis XVI. Even the long-established trade-guilds were dissolved. So deeply imbued were the designers and craftsmen of the day in the Neo-Classic principles, however, that instead of discarding them, they could do no more than interpret them differently, and much that was inherent in Louis XVI design was carried forward, in spite of loud asseverations to the contrary, into the furniture avowedly made to glorify the Revolution and, a little later, the Empire.

Between 1790 and 1800, there was the transitional style known as *Directoire*, though government by the five individuals who made up the Directory actually lasted for four years only, from 1795–1799. The leading French cabinet-maker who developed this manner was Georges Jacob. In form, the furniture is uninterruptedly rectilinear. In mood, it is severe. In inspiration, it is Greek, or Graeco-Roman, but with the emphasis on horizontal rather than vertical lines. Finely figured veneers such as kingwood are displaced by sheer surfaces of mahogany. It is essentially masculine in feeling, and one feels the only women who could be entirely happy with it would be Spartan mothers or those who knitted calmly while heads fell under the guillotine. It is all the more surprising that this rather depressing style should have led, more or less directly, to the English Regency manner, so popular with modern women.

The *Empire* style, from which the Regency largely derives, was an elaboration of the *Directoire*, deliberately contrived to glorify the French Empire and to provide a suitable background for the Emperor Napoleon. Its chief exponents, commissioned by Napoleon himself, were two architects, Percier and Fontaine, who published their *Collection of Interior Decorations* (*Receuil de Décorations Intérieures*) in 1802, a second edition appearing in 1812. During this decade, the *Empire* style dominated, not only France alone, but all the capital cities of Europe, including those with whom Napoleon was at war.

Greek and Roman models continued to be closely copied, and a large contribution by Ancient Egypt resulted from Bonaparte's conquest of the Nile. Sphinxes entire, or their heads only, became one of the favourite motifs—but they were not making their first appearance, for the interest in Egypt was not entirely new, but merely heightened. The sphinx had been used, to a limited extent, on Louis XVI furniture. It now appeared both carved, on the arms of chairs, and cast in metal for the mounts of desks and bookcases.

Much French *Empire* furniture, and some of that made to imitate it, has a funereal splendour that is just the thing for undertakers with delusions of grandeur, or indeed for any tycoon who wants a background that is impressive but a little chilly. I believe the original Woolworth had his study copied exactly from Napoleon's.

To be fair, it isn't all like that. The Grecian-style sofa, of the type made famous by David's portrait of Madame Récamier semi-recumbent upon it, was a most elegant affair. It had a number of variations, but one feature is common to them all—at least one end was in the form of an elegant scroll. Very often, the other end is lower, and scrolled inwards. The feet are sometimes turned verticals, but frequently they are curved in a shape known now as 'sabre', but in fact carefully copied from Greek designs found on decorated pottery. (See Plate XII.)

This use of the scrolled and sabre curves is highly interesting. The designers of the *Directoire* and *Empire* styles deliberately set out to replace the 'decadent' *Louis Seize* with something more severe and serious-minded, but it is hard to escape the conclusion they must soon have reached themselves: that the Louis XVI style had carried the purity of classically straight lines just about as far as it would logically go, and the only way to react from it was to re-introduce the curve, especially for legs. Really, the concave curve of the Empire is the lower half of the cabriole, without the convexity of the knee above. By the time practical cabinet-makers had finished with it, both at home and abroad, the high-minded, forbidding masculinity of the French Empire had softened into a gentle, rather feminine style, with an emphasis on gracious living that recommends it to the modern hostess to whom 'Napoleon' means brandy, and who would probably tell you that Fontaine and Percier were a couple of ballet-dancers.

After the final defeat of Napoleon in 1815, the monarchy was restored, and the more obviously Napoleonic elements of the Empire style ceased to be employed. Its main theme of sober classicism was perpetuated among the middle classes throughout Europe, until about 1850. The history of French furniture after about 1820 is very largely one of revivals—mostly of eighteenth-century styles, but also of the earlier Renaissance periods —Henry II and Henry IV. It is a mistake to think that this process of reproducing the glories of past ages was entirely due to lack of imagination on the one hand, or intention to deceive on the other. Quite the contrary: there was perhaps too much imagination, and it was directed backward. The Restoration of the Bourbons led to a sentimental, nostalgic regard for the monarchy as it had been before the Revolution, and even during the reign (1830–1848) of Louis Philippe, the 'citizen king' who had fought for the Revolution, his royal antecedents seemed more important, at least to the cabinet-makers, than his liberal sympathies, and it became very fashionable to own tables into which were set little porcelain plaques depicting the kings and queens of France. It was a characteristic of these mid-nineteenth-century revivals that they seldom led to the production of exact copies, but tended to mix up elements of different periods in their romantic desire to commemorate the past. (See pp. 145, 147 for a note on the French contribution to the 1851 Crystal Palace Exhibition.)

Britain

Regency or 'English Empire' (1790–1830). Strictly speaking, the

Prince Regent only enjoyed that title for nine years before he ascended the throne as George IV in 1820. The term is extended forward to cover his reign, until his death in 1830, and backward, before the beginning of the century, when French styles, French furniture and French craftsmen were introduced into Britain by the architect Henry Holland. Though France and Britain were almost continuously at war between 1793 and 1815, and Napoleon's domination of Europe made it virtually impossible for English gentlemen to travel on the Continent as they had been in the habit of doing since the days of Charles II, there continued to be a remarkably strong French influence on the design of English furniture.

It is only during the last twenty years or so that Regency furniture has regularly been called 'Regency'. It always used to be known as 'English Empire', meaning the English version of the First French Empire style—and not, on any account, to be confused with the British Empire, now regarded as an antique in its own right.

Your Regency stripes, madam, were an innovation of the *Directoire* style, and were much used in France for draping rooms, perhaps to make them look like the tents of the heroic French army. Their use in upholstery fabric, especially on English furniture, was rather limited, brocade patterns being favoured for this purpose at least as often.

It was not Holland, the professional architect, however, so much as Thomas Hope, an amateur with professional training and an archaeologist, who did more, perhaps, than any other individual to make known the Empire style, in all its romanticized, classically-inspired glory, in England. He himself was most anxious that it should be treated with due respect, and advised discretion in employing it: advice which was not always followed by those, unlike Hope—a man of means—who sought to commercialize the new fashion. Yet it must be admitted, when one compares the ordinary run of Regency furniture with the designs published by Hope himself, that the cabinet-makers of the day tended to exercise far more discretion than he was inclined to do. His house at Deepdene in Surrey was remodelled according to strict principles, based on his knowledge of architecture and archaeology, that he had obtained partly at first-hand, partly through his friendship with the French architect Percier, partly from the publications of the Italian scholar, Piranesi, and those of C. H. Tatham, the protégé of Henry Holland.

Deepdene became a sort of private museum for the housing of genuine antiquities, against a background of furniture and decoration to Hope's own design, in the Graeco-Roman and Egyptian taste. His published designs appeared in 1807, under the title *Household Furniture and Interior Decoration*—just one year later than Sheraton's last work, which tried so hard to keep up with the trend, and which proves, if nothing else, that these ideas were already about before Hope burst into print.

Hot on his heels, in 1808, came a rather more down-to-earth book from a practical and commercially-minded man, George Smith, whose *Collection of Designs for Household Furniture and Interior Decoration* is the most comprehensive record we have of the Empire style, as it was presented to the British public in the early years of the nineteenth century. The way it progressed is to be seen in the plates appearing in Rudolph Ackermann's monthly magazine, *Repository of the Arts*, which provides a running commentary on the development of fashion between 1810 and 1828. Other pattern books appeared in the intervening years, so that the Regency period, as a whole, is extremely well documented, and fairly precise dating is possible, at least in theory.

In practice, it is surprising how much perfectly genuine furniture one comes across that does not have a close counterpart in the design-books; indeed, it is quite difficult to find pieces that conform in every detail to the printed pattern. Apart from academic interest, this is no great loss. A study of the original designs is of the greatest value and interest, but the buyer of furniture for the home is just as well off, in most cases, with the simplified versions produced by the cabinet-makers. In the main, these avoid the extreme exploitation of archaeological detail, and follow the broad outlines of design, achieving a simplicity that is usually far preferable to the studied effects of the pattern-books, and has much more in common with the early Biedermeier style current in Austria, Germany and elsewhere. (See p. 153.)

It is only rarely, for example, that the Regency dining-chair exhibits such features as a leg realistically rendered as that of a goat, or an arm-support in the form of winged griffin. Instead, we have a simple, sabre-leg, and a boldly scrolled arm. The back is invariably low with a straight, or nearly straight, cresting-rail, usually about three inches deep, which may be left perfectly plain, lightly carved or inlaid with brass. Alternatively, the cresting-rail may be in the form of slightly curved bar, carved to represent a rope. Below it, and parallel to it, is a second rail, simply decorated. (See Fig. 23.)

Carving is seldom very elaborate on Regency furniture, as the craft was slowly dying, and there were far fewer carvers available than there had been half a century before. This is perhaps one reason why the more elaborate designs in the books so seldom occur in reality. Marquetry, too, was little practised. Brass was used, rather than ormolu, for raised mounts and also for inlaying, in much the same way that it had been used for Boulle-work. Boulle itself was revived, notably by George Bullock and Louis Le Gaigneur, a Frenchman who set up shop in the Edgware Road.

Mahogany continued in use, but was ousted from fashion by rosewood, imported from Brazil. It is a rich, brown wood with darker markings, and has absolutely nothing to do with the rose-trees in your garden. A wood with an even more pronounced figure in the grain was that called 'zebra', because of its stripe-like markings. Lighter woods such as 'bird's-eye' maple and amboyna, which also has a small, curled marking, fought a losing battle for popularity with the darker ones, which were brought to a fine, glossy finish by French-polishing with shellac dissolved in spirit, applied with a soft pad. This process was introduced into Britain about 1815. It is considered rather smart, these days, to show off one's knowledge by rejecting antique furniture which has been French-polished. Be careful not to overplay your hand by rejecting Regency pieces that were treated in this way when new.

Furniture of the eighteenth century was differently finished, originally, but much of it has been French-polished at some time during the last century and a half, and though this can be a matter for regret, it is not necessarily a sound reason for rejecting an otherwise acceptable piece.

Lacquer was also used to decorate furniture made to meet the latest craze for oriental designs. These were rather more confused than ever before, Chinese, Japanese, and Indian styles co-mingling with Moorish and Egyptian motifs. Brighton Pavilion as it is today is the supreme example of this off-shoot of the Regency style, which confined itself very largely to the whimsicalities of rich men, and left the generality of furniture only slightly affected by it. One oddity which did often creep into everyday pieces was the turning of such things as chair-legs, and the stands of toilet mirrors, to simulate bamboo.

This trick of making one wood look like another was very common. Beech was very frequently got up to look like rosewood or zebra wood.

Gilding was generally limited to the picking-out of carved

FIG. 23

detail on the larger pieces, often used in conjunction with black paint. Black and gold was, in fact, a favourite colour-scheme. Even in the case of the convex mirror, with its circular frame surmounted by an eagle, which became extremely popular, there is usually a reeded black slip between the glass and the completely gilt frame.

These mirrors were usually hung to give, in miniature, a picture of the whole room. In it one might see reflected a circular table about four feet in diameter, most likely of rosewood, mounted on a centre pedestal of substantial proportions, with lion's paw feet. Around it would be a set of sabre-legged chairs, the seats either fully upholstered or with squab cushions resting on cane; against the wall, a bookcase, lower than any made previously, the shelves either open or protected by doors with fine trellises, or *grilles*, of brass instead of glass. Near the fireplace, a chair of the 'bergère' type—in the English sense of the term, with caned sides, back and seat, and loose cushion; facing it, a sofa with scrolled arms and low back, which might even have sprung seats, for springing was now being introduced into upholstered furniture for the first time; at the end of the sofa, a canterbury—a low rack for music, books and newspapers, mounted on casters.

FIG. 23

The early-Nineteenth Century
Empire, Regency and Biedermeier Styles

A. Gentleman's wardrobe in the style of Thomas Hope, with 'Roman' corner-pieces: English, circa 1810.
B. Small sideboard in the Grecian style, with tapering cupboards: English, circa 1810.
C. Sofa-table on 'capstan' base, with splayed feet: English, circa 1815.
D. Standard chair with sabre-legs: English, circa 1815.
E. Elbow chair with sabre-legs: English, circa 1820.
F. Sofa in early *Biedermeier* style, with swan-neck arms: Austrian, circa 1820–1830.
G. Arm-chair in *Empire* style, with sphinx-mounted arm-supports: French, circa 1810.
H. Escritoire with fall-front writing-leaf, in late *Biedermeier* style: German, circa 1840.
I. Chiffonier with grille doors: English, circa 1820.
J. Drum-top table on architectural base, with dolphin feet: English circa 1815.
K. Egyptian motif, after Thomas Hope, 1807.

This is usually constructed with a drawer below and an open framework above, sub-divided, to form the rack. Later versions became very elaborate. That illustrated in Plate XIII is an unusual specimen, with solid sides shaped to fit the lyre-ends. This line is accentuated by the brass inlay, and strings of the lyre are free-standing brass rods. Behind the sofa, we might well find a sofa-table, with fold-down flaps at its ends, supported on a stand which repeats this lyre motif. Alternatively, the sofa-table may rest on a central pedestal, composed of a column descending to a flat platform with a foot, brass-capped and castered, splaying out from each corner. Originally the sofa-table, as its name implies, was intended to be used near a sofa, supporting candlesticks or lamp and writing materials. (See Fig. 23c.)

It is now one of the most popular items in the whole field of antique furniture, but is most often used, today, as a dressing-table, with a toilet-mirror resting on it. Toilet-mirrors were made in large numbers in the late-eighteenth and early-nineteenth centuries, the oval and shield shape frames of the Hepplewhite period giving way, about 1800, to a horizontal, rectangular form, raised on reeded supports above a box-like base containing a couple of small drawers. Don't replace the old glass with modern if you can possibly help it. This applies equally to the full-length 'cheval' mirror, supported between sturdy columns on sabre-shaped feet; the mirror sometimes made adjustable by a system of pulleys and counter-weights, on the same principle, as Sheraton remarked, as a sash window. I recently had one of this type bearing the trade label of the maker, Jackson of Dublin, but was unable to obtain any information about him. There is little available knowledge on the Irish cabinet-makers, which is a great shame, as they produced some fine work. Anyone looking for an interesting field for research might do something very useful in this direction.

The 'gentleman's wardrobe' was an invariable occupant of the late-Georgian bedroom or dressing-room. The example shown in Fig. 23A is characteristic, except that the cupboard above, which is fitted with sliding trays, is higher than usual, one tier of drawers in the lower stage having been sacrificed to give this extra height. The cornice and pediment are a good example of Thomas Hope's Roman style, the curious quarter-circles at the corners being a favourite feature.

Chests-of-drawers of the period are usually straight or bow-fronted, with little or no ornament, beyond a diamond-shaped escutcheon of ivory around the keyholes. Bedroom furniture was almost always of mahogany, the use of rosewood and the other more decorative woods being largely confined to the drawing room, or parlour, with occasional intrusions into the dining-room.

Most dining-tables and side-boards of the larger size were, however, of mahogany. The two- or three-pedestal table was in general use, with the bases becoming increasingly heavy as the nineteenth century advanced. Exactly the same is true of fold-over card-tables. The side-board underwent fundamental changes during the Regency, a reduction of elegance resulting from a reversion to pedestal-cupboards reaching almost to the floor, joined by a flat surface for serving, with drawers in the frieze. The space below was left open for a wine-cooler of sarcophagus shape, tapering downwards. The pedestal-cupboards, too, were sometimes tapered down in the same way, to conform with ideals of Grecian grace (see Fig. 23B). This type of side-board continued to be made for many years and evolved, like the dinosaur, into a monster of frightening proportions, taking nearly as long to die out by becoming too heavy to reproduce itself.

The Victorian side-board developed, with a terrible inevitability, from the severely functional, if rather sombre, classical design of the Regency, to the terrifying edifices of mid-century, backed by massive mirrors and hung with carved swags of dead game, bunches of death-bed grapes and funereal wreaths of flowers and foliage. I suppose the day will come when even these monstrosities will acquire, in someone's eyes, a period charm, but in the meantime it would be nonsense to think of them as a yardstick by which Victorian furniture is to be measured. It would be equally foolish, since it is impossible, to pretend they are not there.

In a horrid sort of way, they are interesting. Even their morbidity exercises a fascination over those who want to know what furniture is *about*, from a historical point of view. I suppose 'romantic' must seem a strange adjective to describe those mighty temples to the great god Roast Beef; but that is only because we have come to use the word to describe third-rate love-stories. Having entitled this chapter 'Neo-Classic to Romantic', I should perhaps make it clear that by 'Neo-Classic'

I mean, quite simply, anything that tries to imitate, well or ill, the architectural and sculptural manner of Ancient Greece and Rome; and by 'Romantic', I mean—rather less simply—anything that tries to take on the glamour, the mystery, the exoticism, of some manner remote in time and place from its own, without accepting the disciplines that governed the original, and without leavening the solemnity of the proceedings with a little native wit. When the Neo-Classic is indulged in without a genuine feeling for its perfection of proportion, and without a touch of humour added to this proper respect, then it takes on the faults of the Romantic movement, and becomes part of it.

The Romantic movement was primarily a literary one, beginning with Horace Walpole's *Castle of Otranto*, published in 1757. Walpole's interest in 'Gothic' styles demonstrates very clearly the way in which the same mood produced both fiction and furniture. It is represented, too, by the works of Sir Walter Scott, whose attitude to history was exactly what I mean by Romanticism, involving a sense of excitement in old battles, a preoccupation with medievalism, a preference for crumbling ruins to well-built houses. Scott carried his romanticism into his own life, furnishing his house, Abbotsford, with an extraordinary collection of ancient relics. Romanticism also involves a certain morbidity, a death-wish such as Keats immortalized when he wrote of being 'half in love with easeful death', and which reached its climax in America with Poe's *Tales of Mystery and Imagination*.

Victorian. So we have our Victorian side-board, a grim reminder of what can happen when people take the past, the present and their own importance all much too seriously.

Fortunately for the Victorians and ourselves, an element of frivolity, a taste for luxury and grace, slipped in through the heavy draperies at the windows, got a cold reception in the dining-room, barely set foot in the bedroom, but finally curled up cosily in the drawing-room. Here, the Rococo, which had been revived in porcelain and silver as early as 1810, began about 1840 to take charge of chairs and sofas, card-tables, work-tables, and mirror-frames. The cabriole leg was back in a Frenchified form, following the academic copying of Louis XIV and Louis XV that took place during the reign of Louis Philippe. (He had lived for a time in England and in America, and both countries were a little inclined to regard him as their *protégé*, and imitate the fashions of his country, if only out of sentimental regard for him personally. He retired to England, following his abdication in 1848, and died there.)

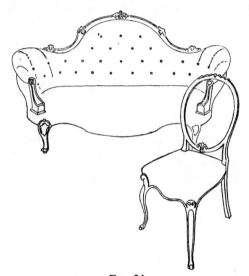

Fig. 24
The Rococo Revival
Early Victorian Sofa and drawing-room chair:
English, circa 1845 to 1860.

Victorian Rococo, however, is impossible to confuse with the eighteenth-century version. It is very much heavier, indulging in such gloriously exaggerated shapes as that illustrated in Fig. 24. Sofas, couches and chairs of this lush, early to mid-Victorian period are very much in fashion again today. Re-upholstered in plushy materials, they certainly have 'style', and there is no doubt that the quality of the frames is often extremely good. Although wood-working machinery was now extensively used, a great deal of the work—the finishing and the assembly, the polishing and the upholstering—was entirely by hand, and the extent to which wood-working machines specifically contributed to the decline in taste from Georgian elegance to Victorian flamboyance is too often greatly exaggerated. Social conditions following the industrial revolution were, of course, greatly influenced by the widespread use of machinery throughout industry, and in that sense, taste and style in furniture were affected. In many ways, machines did something to benefit the furniture industry as a whole, speeding up and reducing the cost of production. This applies particularly to the textiles used for upholstery. The real cause of decline in taste is much harder to pin-point than is often supposed. It is true that the multiplying middle-classes tended to lack the background and taste of the eighteenth-century nobility and gentry: but there had been a 'middle-class' of some importance since Tudor times, and in Victorian England there was still a very powerful ruling class drawn largely from the aristocracy. There seems little evidence that those with an inherited tradition of 'good taste' did much to raise the standard in their own day. On the whole, they seem to have indulged in tastes even more vulgar than those of the general populace. In many a mansion belonging to *l'ancien régime*, fine pieces were pushed away into attics and servants' quarters, to be replaced in the reception rooms by the sort of thing only the *nouveaux riches* are supposed to have liked. The truth is that the dissentients were few and far between, people of all classes admiring and equipping their homes with the newest fashions. Even those with a genuine sympathy for the good things of the past regarded the horrors being produced in their own time as a logical advance and improvement on them. This is clearly to be seen from the writings of Victorian scholars such as Chaffers, who, in his monumental work on pottery and porcelain—still a standard work of reference —praises the work of many contemporary potters who were producing things of such extreme ugliness that it is hard to reconcile their acceptance with an undoubted appreciation of eighteenth-century, and earlier, standards.

In the field of furniture, this confusion of thought reaches its extraordinary climax with the Great Exhibition of 1851. I have recently seen it stated that the exhibits at the Crystal Palace bore little relation to the everyday output of furniture, and this must be accepted to the extent that especially strenuous efforts were made by the exhibitors to offer outstanding pieces. However, there seems no doubt that the same sort of *taste* was operating, and while the judges professed to be applying the highest critical standards, they handed out the prizes to pieces which, in many cases, appear to contradict that principle.

I have before me, as I write, the third volume of the Jury Reports—a magnificent bit of book-binding enclosing 1,332 pages—published in 1852. 'It is important,' says the jury, 'both for the strength and gcod effect of furniture, that the principles of sound construction be well carried out, that the construction be evident, and that if carving or other ornament be introduced, it should be by decorating that construction itself, not by overlaying and disguising it . . . articles of furniture are too often crowded with unnecessary embellishment . . .'

Splendid! They then proceed to give one of the five council medals to M. Fourdinois, of France, for a walnut side-board, which happens to be the only piece of furniture illustrated, and must presumably have been deemed the best thing there. It has all the characteristics of the side-boards referred to a little earlier, and a few more besides. In general style it owes much to Louis XIV Classical-Baroque, but like most Victorian *pastiches* of past periods, it tries at the same time to be an original and contemporary adaptation. In some sense, it succeeds. It includes, in addition to the usual fruit, flowers, mouldings and mirror, six hounds, apparently life-size and carved in the round, chained together; a dead stag, upside-down; six draped females guarding what might be called the third floor; and a similar wench, seated, a little precariously, between the swan-necks of the pediment, with three cherubs on each side of her. This appears alongside the statement that 'articles of furniture are too often overcrowded with unnecessary embellishment.'

Of the five council medals, France took four and Austria, one. Prize medals went to a number of countries, including Sardinia, Tuscany, Prussia and Bavaria—all sovereign states in their own right at that time. The United Kingdom took no less than twenty-two medals. Messrs Burroughes and Watts got one for a billiard-table, Holland and Sons for a carved bookcase, Gillow & Co. for a writing-table.

Gillow of Lancaster, perpetuated today as Waring & Gillow, were one of the leading manufacturers of the time, with an honourable history reaching back to the mid-eighteenth century.

George Hepplewhite himself had served his apprenticeship to this firm. They carried a powerful measure of Georgian tradition into their later work, which is usually stamped with their name, producing some very pleasing, small pieces in the manner of Sheraton. In particular, their bow-fronted, mahogany sideboards on square-taper legs, made in the second half of the nineteenth century, are good enough to be regarded as collectors' pieces.

Indeed, there are many small and medium-size pieces of Victorian furniture which can take their place with dignity alongside the work of earlier periods, and there is a growing fashion for using it in conjunction with modern décor. Those most in demand are upholstered chairs and settees of the revived Rococo, and decorative items such as *papier mâché* tables painted with flowers or landscapes, and inlaid with mother-o'-pearl. The Birmingham firm which made most of this went bankrupt in the 1860's, so that it may be regarded, as a class, as being the best part of a hundred years old.

More attention should be paid, I think, to some of the other things that are largely ignored, at least in Great Britain itself, except by the dealers who are busily exporting them to other parts of the world where their virtues are recognized. The circular table about four feet in diameter, resting on a centre-pedestal, has already been mentioned as a Regency creation. (It may even be regarded as a larger version of the circular tripod-table so popular in the mid-eighteenth century.) It was developed extensively during the Victorian era, being constructed of rosewood, mahogany, and—from about 1850—burr-walnut. The pedestal tended to grow, if anything, rather more elegant in the second half of the century, with a reversion to a cabriole foot splaying out from the central column, in place of the massive trunk, descending to a platform, that had imposing architectural qualities in its Regency form and rather forbidding chunkiness in the early Victorian version. Originally these tables are supposed to have been intended for playing the popular card-game, Loo, and they are still called 'Loo' tables. I have never played the game myself, but I am told it is possible to lose quite a large amount of money at it. Relatively little money need be gambled on the acquisition of such a table. The only part of the world where, so far as I know, there is any great interest in the more ordinary examples is South Africa. More elaborate versions, with tops of inlaid marble, or marquetry often involving a score of finely figured woods, sell at fairly high prices to Italy. English and American buyers are only just beginning to wake up to the advantages of these tables—fine Regency specimens with brass inlay always excepted. Their shape suggests to many people that they need a large room to accommodate them, but this is not so. They seat a surprisingly large number of people, and four chairs can be pushed under them, out of the way. Psychiatrists recommend them, because no one can possibly sit at the head of a circular table. I bought one for myself, as a temporary measure, about fifteen years ago, for nine pounds, and wouldn't want to part with it. We can seat seven people in comfort at it, with the table decently laid.

Dining chairs of the Victorian period are mostly rather heavy and cumbersome. The drawing-room variety, with *ballon*-back, made in sets of six, *en suite* with a sofa, an arm-chair for father and an armless sewing chair for mother, is much more elegant and serviceable (Fig. 24).

The usual Victorian side-board is on the lines of the Exhibition Piece by M. Fourdinois, without the vestal virgins and the pack of hounds but with bags of other ornament and superstructure to compensate. Avoid it like the plague. The English version of the chiffonier, not to be confused with the eighteenth-century French tallboy (see p. 117), is a much better bet. In about 1860 it often took the form of a cupboard about three feet wide, serpentine-fronted, with a drawer and a marble top—excellent for drinks. Many people who find some merit in the chiffonier make the mistake of discarding the mirror above, which is often in a carved frame of elegant shape, and of painting the whole thing off-white, so that it finishes up looking like a make-shift fitment in an impoverished dentist's surgery. In its natural state, the chiffonier is usually of mahogany that has mellowed to what is known as 'fine faded colour', much admired when found in Georgian pieces. To paint it some clinical colour is to make it not better, but infinitely worse. If you are going to have a bit of Victoriana, for heaven's sake don't give it the treatment beloved by Mayfair decorators and women journalists. Have the courage of your convictions—or what Aldous Huxley has called 'the determination of your vices'.

The Victorian chest-of-drawers became very massive, with great thick top and hefty corner posts. It is often of good quality, technically, with well-made drawers of solid mahogany, which is something you seldom find in earlier pieces. Personally, I find the heaviness of design too much to bear, preferring an earlier specimen, even if the drawers are only of pine.

Dressing-tables of the period, wardrobes with mirrors on the outside and marble-topped wash-stands are usually unspeakably hideous. The four-poster bed, that had gone unchallenged in the English bedroom for centuries, gave way for the first time to the half-tester, which has a canopy at the head, supported on scaffolding that would hold up a house and that was concealed by drapes; at the foot was an elaborately framed-up foot-board. Contradicting all I have said above about the folly of messing Victorian pieces about to give them a new look, this is one case where I favour adaptation. The foot-board of a half-tester can very often become a handsome head-board for a modern divan, and many other things—even Fourdinois-type side-board backs—can be utilized in the same way. But do be careful.

After the half-tester came the brass bedstead, to drive the four-poster finally into the lumber-room. The four-poster had undergone little basic change, the only modifications being to the turning of the posts, and the use of mahogany for the finer eighteenth-century specimens, in place of oak. In its basic form, it had withstood every attempt to dislodge it, from a Portuguese style with low footboard introduced in Charles II's time to a Sheraton adaptation of a tented French model of the Louis XVI period. The latter had a head and foot akin to the modern bedstead, but was usually placed sideways against the wall, giving the effect of an enormously deep settee, with the head and foot of equal height, resembling arms.

The modern bedstead of wood with head, foot and side-irons did not emerge in Britain until the end of the nineteenth century, and the first specimens were closely modelled on the form of the brass type. It is odd that it needed this metal episode to bring about a straightforward bed, mainly of wood, that did not tower to the ceiling. Italy had beds remarkably close to modern design, as early as the seventeenth century.

Of brass bedsteads themselves I will say little, except that I don't like them and am entirely out of sympathy with the present revival of fashion which employs them with a nylon net over-drape to produce a sort of 'Baby Doll' atmosphere. They originated during the reign of George IV, but did not become fashionable until mid-century. Technically, there is a difference to be drawn between those made of solid brass strip, and those constructed of brassed tubing. Both types were made in Birmingham.

The nineteenth century produced a wide range of metal furniture of one kind and another. 'Roman' jardinères had been made during the Regency, of cast bronze. Some of the Victorian cast-iron pieces are interesting and usable under present-day conditions. The chief centre of production was Coalbrookdale, more famous for its porcelain. Umbrella-stands cast in the form of a dog or fox, with a riding crop, or sometimes of a cherub with a basket of flowers, seem to go well with yellow front-doors in Chelsea. I must admit I have always wanted, for my garden, one of those marble-topped tables you see in pubs, the legs cast in cabriole shape, the upper section being in the form of human figures. These seem to have originated as propaganda against the slave trade, about 1850, and in early examples of them, the figures are those of negroes. Later ones commemorate historic events, such as the Queen Victoria Jubilees of 1887 and 1897.

These tables are well integrated into the nineteenth century romantic convention in that they tell a story, point a moral, and introduce what was then a present reality into a pseudo-antique form. It is quite misleading to think of romanticism only in terms of the Gothic revival, as this was simply the most obvious expression of it. Much as one hears of Victorian Gothic, it is surprising how little *furniture* of this style one actually sees. Chippendale Gothic furniture is rare, and so is Regency. Good examples of Victorian are far from plentiful. The Gothic revival was largely an architectural one, and against the background of crenulation and stained glass, furniture incorporating many strange styles was placed. Devotees of the Gothic, such as the architect Pugin, did their best to popularize it, but a hotch-potch of mannerisms, ranging from cluster-columns to Moorish arches, and from spiral twists of Charles II style (blandly described as 'Elizabethan') to the heads of Plantagenet kings carved, very badly, in bog-oak—all these went to make up the Victorian Romantic Movement. Most of the results really are rather ugly, but it is foolish to condemn them, as so many critics do, because an uninformed mixture of styles was combined in them. Few furnishing styles were ever 'pure' or 'original'. Most sought their inspiration from ancient models, or from exotic sources. Often these origins were but poorly understood, even during the 'best' periods, as witness the felicitous blending by Chippendale of Rococo, Chinese and Gothic motifs (see Fig. 20). Victorian furniture did not go wrong because it mixed its ingredients, but because it mixed them tastelessly.

The professed reactions against this bad taste were, in themselves, incorrigibly romantic. Following the Paris Exhibition of 1861, English furniture wallowed more happily than ever in the bogus grandeur borrowed from the Second Empire, with its vulgarized Boulle-work mounted in trashy substitutes for ormolu, its overstuffed upholstery, its general attempt to make a drawing-room look like a first-class compartment on a train, and a first-class compartment like a drawing-room. A rebellion against the whole atmosphere, and the methods and way of thinking that brought it forth, was led by William Morris and his friends among the Pre-Raphaelite painters, Rossetti and Burne-Jones. This group attempted, in a practical way, to encourage the design of good furniture, and the making of it *by hand*. Morris was convinced that the decline was mainly due to the use of machinery, and that a return to craftsmanship was the only hope. A certain medievalism was inherent in his attitude and that of those around him. The furniture that resulted forms a curious culmination to the Romantic movement. It is mostly of oak, with hand-made hinges and lockplates of copper or iron and, especially in the commercialized versions that 'the trade' produced, doors of the 'leaded light' type, with panes of coloured glass. The better examples, which are worth acquiring if you can find them, are very plain and surprisingly modern in appearance.

This tradition continued into the twentieth century, with craftsmen such as Gimson and Barnsley producing hand-made furniture of very high quality, mostly in native woods, to severe designs that form a bridge between Gothic Romanticism and the best modern work. Opportunities to see it, much less purchase it, are not frequent. Most of it was made to special order, and many of the finest examples would look odd if divorced from the settings for which they were intended. Artist-craftsmen of the

Morris school never accepted the possibilities of machine-work as an aid to making furniture of good design available to a wide public, and in this respect they were romantics who turned their backs on modern developments, preferring to work in remote Cotswold villages for a few discriminating customers, in the way that the old cabinet-makers and joiners had served their wealthy patrons in the past. It needed Ambrose Heal to extend these principles into the commercial field, and make it possible for furniture-designers to exercise their talents as freely and intelligently as Marot and Cressent, Chippendale and Hepplewhite, Riesener and Röntgen had been able to do in their day, working imaginatively and effectively to suit its conditions. True, the great men had produced things for the privileged minority, but they would have been the first to seize on the advantages of any new aids to production that a mechanical age could offer.

It would be wildly misleading to suggest that the Romantic Movement, led by Morris, was so powerful a force that it swept away the ugliness of late-Victorian furniture with one splendid gesture, clearing the ground for good modern design. In reality it was a minority movement that was limited both in its success and in its outlook. Nor was it the only important departure from the Victorian norm of Neo-Classic, Neo-Gothic, Neo-Baroque, Neo-Rococo and Neo-Everything Else.

One of the most curious styles in the whole history of furniture-design was one which seems to have been invented by a couple of British architects, Voysey and Mackintosh, in the late-Victorian period. The English largely ignored it at first, but adopted it later, after it had found enthusiastic admirers on the Continent, and it subsequently became the sensation of the early 1900's. It is known as *Art Nouveau*, and it was about as new as anything ever can be. It owed a good deal to Japanese art, which was enjoying a great vogue during the so-called 'aesthetic period' that began in the 1880's and lasted about twenty years. This is more clearly to be seen in the decoration than the form of the pieces. Marquetry was used a good deal, sometimes in imitation of Dutch work of the late-seventeenth century, more often in sinuous, rather evil-looking floral patterns. This sinister quality is at its most impressive in the drawings of the only really considerable artist allied to this movement, Aubrey Beardsley, who was greatly influenced by the Japanese colour-print. Painted decoration was also favoured for furniture, bright colours being employed to depict the favourite motifs of the manner—stylized tulips and nymphs in strange postures, clad in swirling draperies. There is an interesting link here with the Pre-Raphaelites attached to the Morris school. Whereas the Pre-Raphaelites were devoted to pure-looking females in chaste drapes, the *Art Nouveau* nymph has a coyly provocative appearance.

The shapes of *Art Nouveau* furniture were not really original, but there was a startling treatment of old forms. Elongation of the kind of curves found in Queen Anne furniture was a favourite trick, so that we find cabriole-legged chairs with narrow seats and high backs, and spidery-looking stands for cabinets. Mrs Beeton, of cookery-book fame, wrote a book in high praise of the new style. By the time it had been adopted by English furniture manufacturers, it had gathered unto it all sorts of extraneous detail, borrowed from every conceivable source, and was far removed from the original intention of Voysey and Mackintosh, who had envisaged something which established a clean break from all the clutter of excessive, irrelevant decoration that characterized the bulk of Victorian furniture.

Edward VII. Out of this extraordinary medley of many styles and conflicting influences there did emerge, at the very end of the nineteenth century, a class of commercially produced furniture that owed little or nothing to *Art Nouveau*, William Morris, or any of the dedicated reformist movements, and yet managed to free itself from the worst excesses of the Victorian convention. It was not at all original, being a revival and adaptation of Sheraton designs. It suffers from a certain insipid quality and a somewhat unimaginative treatment of the standard equipment of a hundred years before—marquetry medallions, square-taper legs, glazed doors neatly divided by astrigals, satinwood painted in the Angelica Kauffman manner. Granted that it is prim and rather uninspired, it yet remains the best-made, most useful furniture with some pretensions to elegance that emerged *in quantity* between the end of the early-Victorian period and the outbreak of the First World War. It is known, generically, as 'Edwardian Sheraton', though it began to appear at the end of Victoria's reign, continued through that of Edward VII and was still being made during the first few years of George V's. It is not really 'reproduction', as many of the pieces have no actual prototypes in eighteenth-century furniture. Card-tables with ingeniously concealed cellarettes, writing-tables that fold down into compact form, Sutherland tables that do likewise, and can be extended to hold a large tea-tray: these are among the many things, made about the turn of the century, that have undeniable merit.

Austria and Germany. The true Empire style of Napoleon's era was adopted throughout Europe (see p. 133) for the furnishing of palaces and great houses, and the results in Vienna and Berlin are not easy to differentiate from those in Paris and London. German interpretation of the classical style was, however, always rather heavy, carcases especially tending to be massive. A geometrical rigidity is especially noticeable in such pieces as secretaires made during the first twenty years or so of the nineteenth century, with very severe cornices of the kind shown in Fig. 23H. Here, the only relief from the uncompromising rectangular shape is provided by the half-circular panel in the fall-front, which is very slightly recessed. Even handles are—most inconveniently—excluded from drawers, so that their flush surfaces shall not be interrupted. To open them, one has to tug the key. We once had a rather pleasing little chest of this type at home, but it had only one key. My wife nearly went mad, moving it from one keyhole to another in order to open the drawers.

After the fall of Napoleon, a simplified version of the Empire style was developed, which became known—though not until it was defunct, a generation later—by the odd and slightly contemptuous name *Biedermeier*. As many German dictionaries do not contain this noun, I will risk appearing patronizing and explain that it means 'a would-be man of honour'. It was used to describe a furnishing style, a school of literature and drama, and a philosophic attitude to life that was compounded of resignation and idealism. It stressed the domestic virtues and the sanctity (its deriders would have said the sanctimoniousness) of family life, and the furniture was made to accord with this solemn outlook. In general terms, it is the Germanic equivalent of English Regency, with certain distinctive differences.

Vienna was the centre of the *Biedermeier* movement, and the characteristics of the style are best observed in Viennese work. While mahogany was extensively used, lighter-coloured woods such as cherry, birch, and maple were also popular. The Grecian style was adhered to rather more pedantically than it was in England, and such welcome eccentricities as settee-arms carved in the form of swans' necks were common. These provided the rolled arm which was an important feature of the style, leading ultimately to the well-stuffed, scrolled arm of the late nineteenth-century 'Chesterfield'. A taste for comfort was already evident in the earliest *Biedermeier* styles, but it was rather inhibited by the insistence on dignity and high-mindedness in the home. (Fig. 23F.)

Dining-room furniture is, at first glance, very like that of English Regency. Side-boards have the Greek sarcophagus-shaped pedestals, and tables are circular, with rather heavy centre-supports. The chairs are stiffer in appearance than English ones of the same date, the legs having a less boldly defined curve. The front legs of *Biedermeier* dining- and parlour-chairs are usually cut rather square, with a slight outward splay. Some of the fine, early examples have a back of lyre form, in the best traditions of Louis XVI, *Directoire*, and Empire classicism.

Such purity gradually deteriorated and, by mid-century, had been corrupted by the Rococo revival. At its best, however, *Biedermeier* was a style of remarkable integrity and of outstanding quality. Very often, in Britain, the fact that it does not conform in every respect to the popular conception of 'Regency' causes it to be rejected. London dealers who cater for continental buyers are far from blind to its possibilities, as these are fully appreciated in Vienna, Berlin, Brussels and Amsterdam. But there remains a great deal that is overlooked, up and down the country, as it was exported to Britain in fairly large quantities when new, and taken there by many refugees who fled from Austria at the time of the *Anschluss*. It is one more answer to those who say that there is no more good antique furniture to be bought at a sensible price.

America. Following the Revolution, there was a movement led by Thomas Jefferson which aimed at establishing a complete break with English traditions in architecture and furnishing. This was not very successful, partly because there was a conservative preference for the things to which people were accustomed (the cabriole leg, for example, and the claw-and-ball foot, persisted in America long after they had ceased to be fashionable in Britain) and partly because the ideal of Roman discipline in design, which the Jefferson school of thought favoured, was also inspiring Robert Adam, George Hepplewhite, Thomas Sheraton, and most other English designers.

The Federal style strove to base itself on French *Directoire* models, with the work of Phyfe (see p. 130) coming, perhaps, nearest to them, but still exhibiting powerful English influence. The Empire manner was earnestly followed, often with great success; its later phase, between 1830 and 1840, draws some of its ideas from the *Biedermeier* styling of legs and arms, and light woods are favoured, as they were in Austria.

At mid-century, the Rococo revival that was twisting European furniture into knots put a positive stranglehold on the parlour-pieces of New York City, where John Belter produced centre- and console-tables with marble tops mounted on stands so burdened with bunches of fruit and flowers that the cabriole legs seem to be bending under the strain. Chairs and settees follow sinuously curving lines, like their English counterparts, but the frames are frequently much more ornately carved and pierced.

The Gothic manner, likewise, reached pinnacles of elaboration unmatched in Europe. Machine production was well under way as early as 1830, and did its damnedest to help every successful business-man to make his entrance-hall look like a cathedral.

In all countries and at all times, certain styles ran concurrently; but nowhere else, and at no other time, were so many conflicting mannerisms evident as in America during the second half of the nineteenth century. The period in which the Civil War was set was also that known to students of interior decoration as the Battle of the Styles. To Neo-Classic, Rococo and Gothic revivals was added another—an outbreak of Baroque based on the most extreme examples of seventeenth-century Italian and Spanish eccentricity, with walnut as the sacrificial material. The Centennial Exhibition of 1878 offered a somewhat misguided corrective with an interpretation of William Morris's medievalism (see p. 150) by Charles Eastlake. Though purporting to be a revival of, and return to, the old crafts, Eastlake's Romanticism was tied to industrialism, and most of the results were largely machine-made. They differed from the other 'reproductions' of the time in that they sought their inspiration in the primitive types made by the early settlers. The cult of 'early American' had arrived.

The authentic work of the early settlers has been described on pages 80 and 81, and its essential similarity to the peasant furniture of Europe noted. Rather than be obliged by chronology to end this book on the depressing discord of international confusion that ruled the city-made furniture of the late-nineteenth century, I have purposely saved till last the agreeable task of writing in more detail about country-made furniture. The chapter that follows will, I hope, come as a relief after this one; but let us not delude ourselves. Our interest in the country cottage, and the furniture of the farmhouse, is essentially romantic and possibly suspect; on that basis, however, our interest in antiques is itself Romanticism. If we cannot escape the charge, let us plead guilty as cheerfully as possible.

CHAPTER SEVEN

Rural Traditions

I т is broadly true to say that the furniture made in rural areas of most countries can be divided into two classes: first, that made in imitation of city styles; second, that which ignored them. This is, of course, an over-simplification, because the two classes overlap each other to a greater or lesser extent, according to the remoteness of the area from the metropolis, the wealth of local residents, the skill of local craftsmen and the staying-power of local traditions.

This last factor is the one I am concerned with in this short chapter. Elsewhere in this book I have tried to give credit to provincial makers who followed city styles at a remove of twenty-five years or so. Their work was often admirable and is of especial interest to the collector of today who cannot afford the high prices that the more luxurious pieces bring. Of equal interest to such a would-be buyer—and not only because it is relatively inexpensive—is the work of the village joiner, who maintained a continuous tradition of slowly changing forms from medieval times until the mid-nineteenth century.

Among the country folk of Spain, Italy, Normandy, and Brittany the *armoire*, under various local names, was still being made, long after the Industrial Revolution had brought mass production to the cities, in much the same way as generations of country craftsmen had constructed it, its doors broken up into small panels by heavy, geometrically arranged mouldings.

Chests—*cassoni*, coffers, mule-chests and dower-chests, all variations on the same theme—were still standard receptacles, being made in 1850 on the same principles that had served in 1650, in villages from Westphalia to Wales.

To understand the peasant furniture of a country it is necessary to live in it. Local traditions, their origins often lost or preserved only in misty legend, govern this or that detail of construction or ornament. It is easy—too easy—to suppose that because a certain earthy, primitive quality is present in all of it, this acts as a common denominator, reducing the entire class of country-made furniture to an easily comprehended craft. This is not so.

The folk-cultures of many countries have much in common, but very much that is not; one has to have a kinship with the place itself before a true appreciation of a Spanish stool, formed from the odd contours of a tree-root, is really possible; the painted furniture of a Swiss farmhouse may appeal to us with its gaiety, but its significance escapes us unless we have experienced the rigours of an Alpine winter, and welcomed the spring as it comes to the valleys.

If it is sometimes difficult to be sure whether a splendid chair or cabinet was made for the *Grand Trianon* or for Windsor Castle, it is because certain styles were, at that level, so cosmopolitan that national characteristics are largely ironed out and are relatively unimportant—except to the scholar who values such information for its own sake, and the dealer who can sometimes make capital out of it.

Differences in peasant pieces are sometimes much more subtle, and there is often no one to explain them. Earnest students of folk-culture unearth a few facts, and then find themselves faced with vast tracts of uncharted territory, undocumented history and ill-founded legend. The dating and placing of much country-made furniture is, if the truth be known, almost anyone's guess.

Fortunately, it is not necessary to know all about a piece of furniture in order to use it and enjoy it; sometimes, the air of mystery that surrounds its origins is part of its charm. From the point of view of the practical home-maker, such difficulties present no real barrier, and if one has chosen to live in a country district, what could be more pleasant than to surround one's self with locally made furniture dating back a century or more? By living in an area, it is possible to acquire a feel for local traditions that is ultimately far more instructive than any book-learning.

Because I attach so much importance to this need for living in a place in order to grasp the true significance of local craftsman-ship, I will largely confine myself to the work of craftsmen in my native Wales, making a few raids across the border into England. Elsewhere in this book I have mentioned Welsh furniture in passing, and the similarity that some characteristic types bear to early American forms. Much that is true of the work of Welsh village joiners applies to their brethren in other parts of Britain and, indeed, to Europe as a whole, but the whole subject of peasant crafts is so fraught with unsuspected dangers that I feel safer by far on my own territory.

'Welsh oak' and, in particular, the 'Welsh dresser' have become by-words among those interested in antique furniture, so that the terms are often applied to things that are not Welsh at all. It is true that oak was used in Wales long after it had ceased to be the fashionable wood in London, but so it was, to only a slightly less extent, in other remote parts of Britain. Ash, elm, beech, sycamore and chestnut were among the other native timbers that were grown, seasoned and made up into joinery by Welsh craftsmen. Walnut was very rarely used, and mahogany was never employed to any extent in Wales until the nineteenth century, when it was cut into veneers to cross-band corner-cupboards and 'grand-father' clock-cases which were otherwise of oak. What sometimes appears to be mahogany is found, on examination, to be oak dyed red with bull's blood. A certain amount of mahogany furniture was made in Regency times at Aberystwyth, Haver-fordwest, and Bangor, but this was in close imitation of London styles, brought at great expense by drover's cart or by sea. It seems to have been cheaper to import furniture from Ireland than from England. With this more sophisticated work I am not concerned here, except to say that Welsh furniture could be very English when it wanted. Most of the time, it just didn't want.

For the rest, traditional patterns were followed with remarkable conservatism. The Welsh forms of the Elizabethan closed court cupboard (see p. 62) are the *cwpwrdd deuddarn* (two-piece cupboard) and the *cwpwrdd tridarn* (three-piece cupboard)—still known colloquially as a *deuddarn* and a *tridarn*. The former follows the two-stage English version very closely, with only the gradual minimizing and eventual disappearance of the turned columns on the upper stage to mark the passage of time. The *tridarn* is, I think, a type peculiar to Wales, having a third deck which is open at the front and was intended to house pewter. Both the *deuddarn* and the *tridarn* are more characteristic of Mid and North Wales than the South. There are, in fact, many important distinctions to be drawn between the different parts of Wales. Until the nineteenth century, there was little traffic between North and South, and even today the mountains present a fairly formidable barrier, the Welsh spoken in the North differing considerably from the Southern idiom. A hundred years ago and more, this lack of communication was much more marked, and it is surprising that it did not make for an even wider divergence in furniture styles than actually existed.

These are most clearly to be seen in the forms which the dresser took, when it began to replace the *cwpwrdd deuddarn* and the *cwpwrrd tridarn* in popularity in the early years of the eighteenth century. It should first be made quite clear that dressers were not peculiar to Wales. Lancashire, Yorkshire and Shropshire all produced recognizable types, with small cupboards set at the ends of the shelves in the upper stage, in the same way as they often are in the Dutch version. Wales is justly famed for its dressers because it made them in greater abundance and variety than did any other country. The attributing of any one variety to a particular area is a little unsafe, but it is broadly true to say that very few of the fine specimens with cabriole legs were made further west than the valley of the River Severn, and without evidence to the contrary, I am inclined to attribute this type to Shropshire. Of Welsh dressers proper, those made in the North usually have a completely enclosed lower stage, with a cupboard each side and a row of drawers down the centre, while the Glamorganshire type has an open lower stage, consisting of drawers in the frieze and a pot-board below. What, then, is one to make of the extraordinary piece illustrated in Plate XIV? This is a corner-dresser from West Wales and is composed of one half conforming to the Northern, closed form and the other resembling the Southern, open type. Corner-dressers were at one time fairly common in Pembrokeshire and Cardiganshire, but very few seem to have survived. Most of them were built-in fitments, and have been torn out in the course of the redecoration and moderniza-tion of farmhouses. The more usual type of dresser from West Wales is still fairly plentiful, and this, too, effects a compromise between North and South, having a row of drawers in the frieze, and two doors fitted to the lower stage, with an open space between them. So far as one can judge, this arrangement is a fairly late development which began in the early nineteenth century, and there is a certain lack of character in many speci-mens that suggests they were produced in large quantities to a fixed pattern. Quite probably, some are not truly Welsh at all, but importations from Bristol, brought by ship to Milford Haven.

The dating of dressers is even more tricky than placing their probable district of origin. North Welsh specimens with Gothic arched panels to the doors can usually be accepted as eighteenth century, as can South Walians with well-turned columns in the lower stage and arched aprons. Cock-beading on the drawers suggests a date not later than 1820, and not earlier than 1750. Later specimens usually lack the refinement of cock-beading, whereas earlier ones have a curious chamfering of three sides of the drawer—the top edge being left plain. Shaping of the ends of the upper stage is a pleasant feature but is no safe indication as to date. Hand-made cup-hooks of wrought iron were in regular use until the middle of the nineteenth century.

Not all dressers were of oak. In the eighteenth century, and to a greater extent in the nineteenth, some people with a little extra money to spend kept up with the fashion by having their dressers made of mahogany. This was far from being a general practice, however, and mahogany dressers are comparatively rare. North Wales has more to offer than any other district.

At the other end of the social scale, those who could not afford oak, or who wanted to be different, had dressers of pine. It is a mistake to think of pine as being, necessarily, a cheap substitute for hard woods. When it first came to be used extensively, under the name of deal, in the seventeenth century, it was highly regarded and not particularly cheap. It is a very pleasing timber, and when stripped of paint, varnish, stain and any other surface coating, it can be waxed up to a really beautiful colour. Dressers, chests—even kitchen tables—respond very well to this treatment.

'Farmhouse-refectory' tables of severe design are still to be found, but are becoming scarce. They are usually about eight feet in length and two feet nine inches in width. The top is detachable from the stand, which usually has four square legs about four inches thick. The edges of the legs are sometimes relieved by a 'stopped chamfer'—the right-angle is shaved off for the greater part of the length, but left alone at top and bottom. The tops of these tables are often of elm, and should be carefully checked for worm. A thorough treatment with a good insecticide on the underside is usually one hundred per cent effective.

Rectangular flap-tables, opening up to a size large enough to seat six or eight people, were a usual addition to the Welsh farm parlour in the late eighteenth century. They are invariably of oak, but English counterparts in mahogany, of the type that formed the central section of the 'D-end' table, are also to be had.

A characteristic Welsh type is the circular cricket-table, so-called because of its three stump-like legs. It is normally about two feet six inches in diameter, and occurs in two main forms. One has rounded legs which peg into the underside of the top, in the way that a milkmaid's stool is constructed, and splay outwards. They are joined below by similarly rounded stretchers. This type is usually of ash. The second type of cricket-table is of oak and is more elaborately constructed, the legs being of square or triangular section, with an under-tray uniting them (Fig. 25). Both types are traditional and difficult to date, but 1760-1820 is about the span.

Welsh chairs are usually simplified versions of English types, but may well be half a century behind the times. Queen Anne styles were still current in 1760, and hard-seated, square-backed Sheraton models were, to my certain knowledge, still being produced in 1840. They are none the worse for that. Usually of fruitwood—apple or pear—stained to simulate mahogany, they go to prove that good taste survived rather longer in Wales than it did in most other places. Not only were the Welsh slow to accept new designs and integrate them into their tradition; they were reluctant to part with their possessions, or even to move them from one house, or from one room, to another. I have known the heavier pieces, such as the enormous chests with coffered lids made on medieval lines to store grain, that have been standing so long in one position that they have been infected by dry rot—an affliction which usually overtakes constructional timbers of houses only. Even the 'coffer bach' ('little coffer') tends to remain, very properly, undisturbed for generations.

Returning to the subject of chairs, there are three types that I have seen in Wales and nowhere else. The Bardic chairs awarded at the annual Eisteddfod are purely romantic. The beehive chair is made of basketwork, like the coracles made for the fishermen of West Wales. It has a very ancient history indeed, dating back to the time of the Roman occupation of Britain. It has a draught-excluding, domed back, which finds a continental counterpart in an upholstered type of similar shape that was made in France in the eighteenth century.

The other kind of chair which, so far as I know, is peculiarly Welsh usually follows the Chippendale square-legged pattern of about 1760. It has a simply pierced splat and open arms, such as you will find on any 'farmhouse Chippendale' chair. The unusual feature is a drawer placed under the seat. This has been variously explained to me as intended (*a*) for the family Bible or (*b*) for pipe, tobacco, and anything else the master of the house might need for his creature comforts after a long day on the hill-side, rounding up the sheep.

FIG. 25

Cottage Furniture

Welsh 'Cricket' table and Windsor Chair,
late eighteenth century.

Welsh furniture is just that little bit different from everything else, and for that country cottage you want to buy when you retire, it's the ideal thing.

A more popular choice for countrified furnishing schemes is the ladder-back chair, usually associated with Yorkshire but made in many parts of Britain. The original ladder-backs were simply constructed of ash, beech or oak, with rush seats. The rungs of the back are thin in section, and slightly curved. They are extremely useful in that they take up little space, but they are inclined to be top-heavy and, if in not very good condition, a little rickety. It is not always easy to get the seats re-rushed when they need it. It is interesting to note that the fine mahogany ladder-back chairs of the Chippendale period drew their inspiration from these country specimens, instead of the other way round; but perhaps it is not surprising when one considers that Chippendale was a Yorkshireman.

One of the best-known and best-loved items in the whole range of antique furniture is the Windsor chair, and there could be no better subject for the final paragraphs of a book of this kind. Its origins are uncertain, but there was certainly an industry flourishing in the New Forest in the early 1700's. Oak was hardly ever used. Elm was the standard timber for the seat, beech for the legs and spindles, ash or yew-tree for the hooped back. In the later eighteenth century, a rail of comb-shape often took the place of the traditional hoop. During the 'Chippendale Gothic' period, the hoop was forced into the form of a pointed arch, and cabriole legs took the place of the usual turnings. Under-stretchers and arms supports are often of bent wood on· examples made prior to 1820. After that date, turnings grew heavier, and the craft that had been carried on in the forests, with a live sapling providing tension to drive the lathe, moved very soon into the first furniture factories to be set up in High Wycombe. Not all the craftsmen deserted the woodlands, however, and in the present century, men still worked among the trees, cutting them and fashioning them into the traditional Windsor chairs.

Find one with a well-shaped back to rest the shoulders, fit a cushion to the elm seat. Place it at your fireside, and rest content.

Index

INDEX